TRAVEL WRITING

A Practical Guide

Benin artist Claude Adamasou, one of the many fascinating
individuals who has inspired the author to write – *see* page 12.
(Photo: Annie Caulfield)

TRAVEL WRITING
A Practical Guide

ANNIE CAULFIELD

THE CROWOOD PRESS

First published in 2007 by
The Crowood Press Ltd
Ramsbury, Marlborough
Wiltshire SN8 2HR

www.crowood.com

British Library Cataloguing-in-Publication Data
A catalogue record for this book is available from the British Library.

ISBN 978 1 86126 959 1

Typeset by S R Nova Pvt Ltd., Bangalore, India

Printed and bound in Spain by Graphy Cems

Contents

ACKNOWLEDGEMENTS

With many thanks to the following:

Peter Moore at www.petermoore.net for permission to quote from his Amazon Short, *Same Same but Different*; Pluto Press for permission to quote from *Staying Power: The History of Black People in Britain* by Peter Fryer (1984); Sheil Land Associates for permission to quote from *The Blind Leading the Blind: A Century of Guidebook Travel* by Alan Sillitoe, Macmillan UK, 1996; *On Bullfighting* by A.L. Kennedy published by Yellow Jersey, 1999, reprinted by permission of The Random House Group Ltd; quotation from *Looking For George* by Helena Drysdale, 1996, with permission of Pan Macmillan and A.P. Watt Ltd, copyright Helena Drysdale, 1996; quotation from *The Sun In My Eyes* by Josie Dew, 2001, reprinted with permission of Little Brown Book Group; quotation from Barry Turner, *The Writer's Handbook 2007*, with permission of Pan Macmillan, copyright Barry Turner, 2007.

For my mother, who never lets anything defeat her.

INTRODUCTION: WHAT IS TRAVEL WRITING?

In a bookshop, novels are shelved under novels, biographies under biography and children's books under children's books – but travel writing? Sometimes there is a section called 'Travel Literature'; some bookshops classify these volumes under 'Travel Memoirs', while others slot travel writing in beside guidebooks to the appropriate country.

But what is this form of writing? Putting books of travel writing alongside the guidebooks may be a good idea. These books are a complement to a guide-book, not a substitute. The guidebook is the map; the travel writing volume is the interesting companion you've chosen to take on your journey. I was about to say an 'interesting and amiable companion', but some great travel writing is written by very irritable souls. Bill Bryson and P.J. O'Rourke would disap-point if they did not argue with someone on their reported journeys.

In Bryson's confrontations with the world's pedants, jobsworths and mean-minded employees of service industries, it often seems he's living out a fantasy on behalf of the rest of us. So often we've wanted to explode into an angry tirade in an airport, hotel reception or car hire office, but have slunk away muttering to ourselves, fuming inside with our wrongs not righted. To read Bryson's explosive verbal attacks on people who seem to have been put on earth to irritate travellers is cathartic as well as amusing. He says the things we wish we'd said. He makes it clear that a cheery, accepting disposition is not a prerequisite on a journey, nor in travel writing.

P.J. O'Rourke is a good writer for woolly liberals like myself to read. He goes out into the world and crossly asks 'Why?' when confronted with the mindlessly politically correct, or the half thought-out schemes of the well-intentioned. O'Rourke forces readers who don't agree with him to think hard-er about their opinions. Numerous times I've found myself having silent arguments with O'Rourke as I read his books – sometimes I win, sometimes I feel foolish, but I do feel that I finish his books a little wiser.

O'Rourke is really a provocative journalist, but his investigations take him far and wide. He's an example of how flexible the travel writing genre can be. Perhaps some would argue that he is more of a reporter and shouldn't be included, but for an insightful snapshot of a country he is someone I would refer to. O'Rourke often writes around his main investigation to give a broader picture of the place he's visiting. He may be reporting on a war, but his acerbic cultural observations and quick summarizing of a country's history or political situation make his pictures of a place vivid beyond reports from a correspondent.

THE WRITER'S CHARACTER

The entertaining travel writer is not necessarily the person you would want to be travelling with in real life. But on paper, he or she is interesting to observe. The writer who is a competent traveller, never meeting with mishap, self-doubt, irritation or even disaster could find their books are merely slim volumes of bragging.

In his essay *Stranger on a Train*, Paul Theroux writes of how uncomfortable, lonely, exhausting and frustrating travelling can be. He suggests that the often unpleasant isolation of a journey can produce insight into oneself as well as one's surroundings. Being forced into the difficulties that are inevitably part of travel contributes to the writer's real task, to discover something about human nature. New insights into life are provoked by travel. Travelling to a strange place gives a new perspective on the place one has left behind and on the person one had assumed oneself to be when comfortable and secure at home.

A travel writer's character is at the heart of their style. As with actual companions, they vary widely in personality type. Taking a liking to them, or disliking them, depends on your own personality type. Some writers are more amusing than informative. Some have specialist knowledge that leads to an unusual insight into a place. Some simply have more acute powers of observation and can notice the way the evening light catches an ancient monument in a way the rest of us would never see without the writer to point it out, and point it out with a gift for finding the exact, fresh, descriptive words.

THE NATURE OF TRAVEL WRITING

There is no real format for writing travel books. They vary almost as much as people vary and are certainly as various in style as novels. Even when travel writers try to keep themselves in the background their books still bear the stamp of their personality. Sven Linqvist's intellect and sensitivity glow through the self-effacing accounts of his journeys. The energetic recklessness of Redmond O'Hanlan accompanies a specialist scientific knowledge to make his writing unmistakable. Similarly there is the sporty cheeriness of Josie Dew; the voluptuousness of Bruce Chatwin; the considered restraint of Jan Morris; the robust humour of Peter Moore; the tough courage of Robyn Davidson – the travel writer is part of the story.

No matter how little the writer puts themself into the story, their interests, cultural background, temperament and areas of expertise influence even the very choice of destination. It is the job of the sociologist, historian, anthropologist or journalist to attempt objectivity; in a travel writer this objectivity would be like having dinner with someone who will only discuss the menu. I once taught a journalist on a travel-writing course; this was interesting for me because it clarified where travel writing and journalism differ. In a morning seminar the journalist distracted us all with an incongruously funny story about being taken, at gun point, to meet a terrorist leader who disliked an article he had written. He remembered standing in a hideously decorated room, looking at nasty yellow curtains and a Draylon sofa – the furnishings making it all seem squalid and undignified more than terrifying. His emotional description, full of detail, humorous asides and honest description of fear, vanished when he came to put the story on paper. There were no nuances of feeling, no jokes and no yellow curtains. There was minimal scene setting and no hint of the writer's opinion. For years he had been trained by editors to cut out the extraneous detail. In what he wrote I could hear the newspaper editor shouting, 'I don't want all this! Who was the terrorist leader? What did he say? Why did he let you go? Just give us the facts. Do *not* tell us about the yellow curtains!'

But travel writing is about the yellow curtains. Travel writing is the detail behind and beside the news. It does include those inconsequential fragments of observation that add together to make a full picture of a person, place and moment in time. Travel writing includes personal feeling, to lift a piece beyond a catalogue of facts, transforming it into an invitation to the reader to come along on the journey.

Is travel writing like novel writing? A little, just as it is a little like journalism. Not all the information in a travel book serves the interests of the story, although there is often a story told. A reader can get the flavour of a place just as well in a novel or a play, but a travel book is more likely to have facts woven into the narrative, atmosphere and characterizations. Novels let the reader know how the world feels emotionally, but may not convey facts through the storytelling. Travel writing uses all the tricks of storytelling to lure the reader in, with the added incentive that this is a true (more or less true) story that will tell the reader something concrete about the world. I say more or less true, because, leaving aside occasional characters who did completely make up tall tales of their adventures, travel writing edits, polishes and selects facts. *The Road to Oxiana*, Robert Byron's tale of his journey through Afghanistan in 1933, reads like spontaneous jottings in the diary of a man in a hurry. The reader is on the breathless journey with the funny, argumentative, learned adventurer. There are vivid moments of exasperation, hilarity, awe, terror and boredom with every turn of the page. Yet Byron carefully edited his notebooks for three years to create the lively effect he wanted.

One could probably find Robert Byron's original notebooks in a museum collection somewhere. They might be interesting historical documents for a scholar working on Robert Byron, but they would hardly be the average person's notion of a good read. Similarly, if one wanted to study Afghanistan in 1933 it might be better to go to a newspaper archive of the time, or to find a good history book on the subject. But for a sense of how it felt to be in Afghanistan in 1933, the travel writer is the source to turn to.

Robert Byron was a great believer in leaving behind fancy travel equipment and taking a few good books and several bottles of claret. He loathed the career-minded, athletic or scientific traveller – and wanted simply to hear the opinions of a well-read, ordinary, affable man who had made a journey. In the observations of this ordinary man with his rucksack full of wine and literature, Byron felt the truth about a country would be found.

Byron may have been a little self-deprecating in his insistence on this. His own meanderings with wine and literary knowledge to hand, come alive on paper because he has an insight, courage and humour that are far from ordinary. Who Robert Byron was before he set out with his wine, books and notebooks determined the resulting manuscript more than he admitted.

OTHER DEFINITIONS OF TRAVEL WRITING

Is travel writing a form of autobiography? This depends on how personalized the writer's style is, and on the nature of the story. Certainly part of the fascination of travel writing is the glimpse into a moment in a real person's life. The moment may be edited and polished in its expression, but it is not fancy – someone did these things, in this place for real. In the introductory note to his intriguing story *Books, Baguettes and Bedbugs*, Jeremy Mercer writes that he found truth becoming 'liquid' when recalling his time in Paris. He admits that chronologies were altered and events 'distilled' or 'condensed' in order to make a shape out of that period of his life. But how else would he have fitted the story into a reasonable number of pages and given it a structure?

'Distilling' and 'condensing' are as good a description of the process of making a travel book as any I have found. The truth is 'liquid', as it would be when writing an autobiography, but it should still be the truth.

In his essay on travel writing *The Journey and the Book*, Johnathan Raban suggests that writers like the contained shape of a journey. It is a memory with a beginning, middle and end, like a childhood. Selecting what is important and what can be discarded from the recorded version of the memory is the real job of the travel writer. The journey itself is just a small part of the travel writer's work.

I would add to this that there is nevertheless a skill in selecting the journey, in knowing what is likely, for a particular writer, to create a vibrant, significant memory to turn into words. The process of choosing the right journey is discussed later in this book.

THE FUTURE?

Some people wonder whether travel writing has a future in this age of easy travel, to even the most far-flung places. Armchair travellers have a wide range of television documentary channels to watch. Do we need travel books at all? Publishers still buy travel books. Bookshop owners are still making decisions about where to place those pesky travel books on their shelves. And very occasionally a travel book is on the non-fiction bestseller lists alongside the lives of footballers, their wives and their ex-lovers. So it would seem the travel writing genre is far from dead. Film and television drama have not done away with the need for the intimate experience of reading a novel; so the documentary does not cancel out a need for the personal voices of travel writers. Not everyone likes to travel with a crowd; they like to be with one person they trust. If everyone can travel cheaply, why read about it? For one thing, travel might be cheaper to many places but it still isn't free. And there are trips to more inaccessible places that cost a small fortune for those who would have to pay their own way. Although there are a multitude of places cheaply and easily reached these days, the traveller might not have the writer's expert knowledge, courage, sociability, energy or ability to meet with comic disaster. People might read about places they will travel to for added insight. They might read about places they will never go because they haven't the time, the good health, the money or the inclination to endure long flights. People might read about a place they once travelled to in order to relive precious experiences, to rediscover half-remembered sights, smells or possibly to enjoy tossing the book aside in violent disagreement with the author.

This is an overcrowded market because being a travel writer is such a pleasurable way to live. Travel writers are seldom rich in anything but experience. Sustaining a career can take some ingenuity. Nevertheless, travel writers continue to write; their books continue to be bought. Even very old volumes of travel writing continue to sell because, although a book may be out of date, it is still readable. Travel writing gives us a portrait of a place and its people at a specific time. For example, Helena Drysdale's book about her journeys in Romania, *Looking for George*, shows Romania before and after Ceaușescu. The country changes completely in the space of a decade. Accounts of her earlier travels are there to explain the pools of darkness she encounters in the more liberated, later Romania.

To write *Irish Blood, English Heart, Ulster Fry*, I travelled in Northern Ireland in 2004, recalling other journeys taken in the 1990s, 1980s, 1970s and 1960s. Each time the country was different. The final journey was taken when the country was in an unusual mood of optimism. Perhaps someone reading the book ten years from now may see the optimism was momentary and mistaken. But for me, that is the fascination of travel writing; it provides detailed pictures of countries at particular times. Those countries may never be the same again. The politics, the culture, the climate, the wildlife, the boundaries, the economy of a country might have changed drastically ten minutes after a book had been written – but how it seemed, at a specific moment, has been recorded.

People too are recorded in travel books. The people encountered on a journey are only on the earth for a short time. A whole race and their way of life could be systematically destroyed. In *Return to the Marshes*, Gavin Young describes a people, the Madan of southern Iraq, descendants of the Sumerians, who were almost wiped out by Saddam Hussein. A way of life could simply be dying for economic reasons, as witnessed in Redmond O'Hanlan's *Trawler*, where deep sea fishing is beginning to prove too dangerous and costly for the fishermen to keep going. Perhaps a travel writer comes across an individual living in what, for them, are simply ordinary circumstances but that seem to the outsider to be a stunning display of human fortitude, eccentricity, altruism or ingenuity. A travel writer notices what these people, who never made the news and may never make the history books, were doing on the day the writer came across them in their particular landscape.

> There was no possibility of teaching art – the nearest school was in the Ivory Coast and Benin's schools thought sport was a more important subject to put on the timetable. Claude subsidized his painting income by coaching football at local schools. His father had worked as a cartographer in local government after he came to Cotonou, and before that he'd driven trucks. He'd preferred the truck driving as it enabled him to travel, to see things and sell his paintings in new markets.
>
> Claude's studio was a table in one of his two rooms. He took off his shirt and put on the stripy apron he wore for work – this was his wife's idea, as she had threatened to divorce him after a week if she had to keep washing paint out of his clothes.
>
> 'I'm doing a big card so you can see the strokes. Also, I want you to see it's really me that does these paintings, I don't sell them at double the price for the real artist.' By coincidence, as Claude began painting at his heavy wood table in front of the window, an unusually cloudy sky cleared so the sun poured in.
>
> 'He's all lit up', Isidore said. 'Do you see? Not just the sun – as he starts to work he's happy.' Claude smiled. 'Very true. I can do this for hours. Ah really, my father gave us a great inheritance. As he taught us to paint he said it probably wouldn't make us rich but it would give us infinite pleasure in being alive.'
>
> Annie Caulfield, *Show Me the Magic* (Viking Penguin, 2002)

Travel writers go into the world and record people, landscapes and cultures that may never be found again. They shine a light on people and places exclusive to their personal point of view; a point of view we can trust or distrust, like or dislike, in exactly the way we would judge the opinions and observations of a travelling companion. And the great thing is, we are not stuck in a hotel room with the travel writer – if we don't enjoy their company, we can close the book.

One Travel Writer Explains Herself

Those who venture to add a new volume to the vast literature of travel, unless they be men of learning or politicians, must be prepared with an excuse. My excuse is ready, as specious and I hope as plausible as such things should be. I desired to write not so much a book of travel as an account of the people whom I met or who accompanied me on my way, and to show what the world is like in which they live and how it appears to them. And since it was better that they should, as far as possible, tell their own tale, I have strung their words upon the thread of the road, relating as I heard them the stories which shepherd and man-at-arms beguiled the hours of the march, the talk that passed from lip to lip around the camp-fire, in the black tent of the Arab and the guest-chamber of the Druze, as well as the more cautious utterances of Turkish and Syrian officials.

Gertrude Bell, *The Desert and the Sown* (Heinemann, 1907)

TRAVEL WRITING PAST, PRESENT AND FUTURE

Early Travellers

Who the first inhabitants of Britain were, whether natives or immigrants, is open to question: one must remember we are dealing with barbarians. But their physical characteristics vary, and the variation is suggestive. The reddish hair and large limbs of the Caledonian proclaim a German origin; the swarthy faces of the Silures, the tendency of their hair to curl, and the fact that Spain lies opposite, all lead one to believe that Spaniards crossed in ancient times and occupied that part of the country. The peoples nearest to the Gauls likewise resemble them. It may be that they still show the effect of a common origin; or perhaps it is climatic conditions that have produced this physical type in lands that converge so closely from north and south. On the whole, however, it seems likely that Gauls settled in the island lying so close to their shores. In both countries you find the same ritual and religious beliefs. There is no great difference in language and there is the same hardihood in challenging danger, the same cowardice in shirking it when it comes close. But the Britons show more spirit: they have not yet been enervated by protracted peace. History tells us that the Gauls too had their hour of military glory; but since that time, a life of ease has made them unwarlike: their valour perished with their freedom. The same has happened to those Britons who were conquered early; the rest are still what the Gauls once were.

Tacitus [AD55–c.118], *Agricola and Germania* (trans. H. Mattingly and S.A. Handford, Penguin Classics, 1973)

Who was the first travel writer? I suspect travel writing began with language. The first man able to tell a tale came home and told his fellow cave dwellers what he had seen while out hunting that day. Just as children are asked, 'What happened at nursery school today?', an essential part of learning to communicate, it would seem, is to tell a tale of journey to another place.

'Being torn apart by bears was only one pitfall of travel in the Victorian age ...' [Alan Sillitoe, *The Blind Leading the Blind: A Century of Guidebook Travel (1815–1911)* Macmillan UK, 1996].

Travel was once much more difficult than it is now – physically arduous and in many places, dangerous. Travel was slow and isolating in the days before airmail, telephone and email. Yet in some ways it was easier, if you wanted to make up fantastic tales of monsters seen and perils survived, who was going to rush to follow in your footsteps and contest your claims? There were times before film, before photographs, when the only evidence required was what your pen produced. It was also possible, in the days of conquest and empire, to carry the prejudices of your culture around without any need for honest reappraisal in light of the facts.

To See Ourselves ...

The historian Basil Davidson points out that it was not until after World War II, with the collapse of empires, that some truth about Africa began to emerge. Until then, there had been a view from the outside that Africa had no history of its own. There was perceived to be no indigenous culture or civilization. It was widely assumed that before the arrival of Europeans there had been nothing in Africa but a dark, savage wilderness.

At various times in history, from various external viewpoints, England, France, Ireland, South America, Australia – most places – have all been dismissed as places without civilization, with a population of human beings lumped in with the country's fauna. Recently this dismissive, external view has come from Europe, but going further back in time, to the writings of older empires, the pattern remains the same. The Islamic empire viewed most of Europe as a place in need of civilizing and before that the ancient Romans viewed northern Europe as a place of savagery and bad weather. In his book, *Exterminate All The Brutes*, Swedish author Sven Linqvist points out that the word 'Europe' derives from a Semitic word that means 'darkness'.

These external views are dismissive because they come from the conquering power of the time. As the saying goes, history is written by the victors. So too, most of the travel writing comes from the wealthier and more dominant cultures of a time. Thus it is chastening to read the views on the rest of the world from the present-day United States of America and to realize that, although not deemed to be living entirely in primeval darkness, it seems we are at best quaint eccentrics with bad teeth and at worst in need of a civilizing invasion of some kind.

Looking at Others

In an edition of *National Geographic* magazine, published around the time of the 2006 World Cup, I was astonished at an American soccer enthusiast's descriptions of the game we Europeans know as football. He observed us fondly, admiringly even, as we went about our worship at the shrines of our strange sporting cult. It occurred to me when I finished reading the article, that the most powerful nation on earth doesn't play a sport that the rest of us, even bookish girls, understand to be an essential part of life. And because they are the most powerful nation on earth, they describe us footballing peoples as the quaint ones. It was an odd feeling to read about myself as one of the 'other' people of the earth. Although in a far more trivial context, it reminded me of the sensation Chinua Achebe described as he read and enjoyed Conrad's *Heart of Darkness*. It suddenly occurred to him that he wasn't with the protagonists on the boat – he was one of the shadowy figures in the jungle firing arrows across the water. It reminded me of how easy it can be in travel writing to simply make the people observed into, 'the others'.

Reading back into the travel writing of the Victorians, or back further to the Elizabethans or the Crusaders, we are often shocked, impatient of ignorance and able to spot any number of downright lies. The assumption of the writer being from a superior people to the observed is not only assumed but backed up with nasty fabrications. In his book, *Staying Power: The History of Black People in Britain*, Peter Fryer quotes several early travel writers, including Sir Thomas Herbert who visited Africa in 1627: 'Their language is rather apishly than articulately founded, with whom 'tis thought they have unnatural mixture ... Having a voice 'twixt humane and beast, makes that supposition to be of more credit, that they have a beastly copulation or conjuncture.'

Herbert also claimed to have witnessed Africans not only enjoying eating each other but being eaten:

> Not satisfied with natures treasures ... the destruction of men and women neighbouring them, better contenting them, whose dead carcasses they devoure with a vultures appetite; whom if they misse, they serve their friends (so they mis-call them) such scurvy sauce, butchering them, thinking they excuse all in a complement, that they know no rarer way to express true love than in making (not two souls) two bodies one in an inseparable union: yea, some (worne by age, or worme-eaten by the pox) proffer themselves to the shambles, and accordingly are jointed and set to sell upon the stalls.

Sad to say, Herbert was not some lone lunatic but voiced opinions often repeated at the time of slavery and early British colonialism. These old travel writings are essential reading to show us attitudes of the time. In those of travel writers of the past we can see how the people of a particular time thought about the world beyond and how those thoughts enabled them to do things that seem appalling to us today. Reading about old attitudes and assumptions can lead us through history to explain why many parts of the world are still reeling, damaged and struggling to enter the world on an equal footing. Old travellers' tales help us to trace back the racial stereotyping and prejudices that still haunt the structures and attitudes of today's world. In these post-colonial days we would expect travel writers to be more accurate, thoughtful and culturally sensitive. This is not always the case. The notion of the inefficient, comical foreigner still crops up in travel literature as much as the notion of the alluring exotic maiden or the noble savage. Generalizations about a people, for example, 'Iraqis are ...' or 'Most Nigerians ...' still occur.

White people of European origin still make up most of the writers travelling the world and observing. They are seldom the observed. A book like Caryl Phillips's *The European Tribe* in which a Caribbean man looks around Europe remains a rarity. An African returning to Africa, in a travel memoir such as Ekow Eshen's *Black Gold of the Sun*, brings a new layer to travel writing and suggests that the form is shaking itself up, shedding new kinds of light on the world. In the work of the Swedish writer Sven Linquist poetic meditations on the European colonial past suggest why both the young adventurer having a lark abroad or the white person on a civilizing mission have demonstrated a dangerously irresponsible trend in travel writing and have backed up some of the atrocities of history. In *Desert Divers*, he writes about how European adventurers and explorers behaved in the Sahara – Loti, Saint-Exupéry, Vieuchange, Eberhardt and Gide in particular. They sought escape from the inhibitions of their own society and fled domestic boredom to indulge in exploits that included child abuse, sexual excess and complicity in terrible violence being perpetrated on their behalf. They could live out their wildest fantasies against an exotic North African backdrop, without fear of social disgrace.

Sometimes writers told of their travels and helped to build up a body of evidence against the prevailing regime, ideology and culture. Their work spread the news to the folks back home that terrible things were being done in the name of civilization. These works provide readers today with an insight into why certain practices, beliefs and the shocking evidence of traumas remains in societies where brave Europeans once adventured in search of fortunes. Travellers' tales told of the worst excesses of imperialism and sometimes helped to end them.

The Swedish missionary Edward Sjoblom published a book called *In the Shade of the Palms* in 1907. It tells of his growing horror regarding the behaviour of white men in the Congo. His work was rescued and quoted in *Exterminate All the Brutes*, a chilling piece of travel writing by Sven Linqvist. At one point Sjoblom is giving a sermon in his Congo church. He is interrupted when a soldier seizes an old man, accusing him of not having collected enough rubber. Sjoblom asks the soldier to stop, or to at least wait until the service was over. The soldier ignores him, drags the old man another few feet away, puts a gun to his head and shoots him. Sjoblom concludes his account of the incident: 'A small boy of about nine is ordered by the soldier to cut off the dead man's hand, which, with some other hands taken previously in a similar way, are then the following day handed over to the commissioner as signs of the victory of civilization.'

Sjoblom's work was taken up by anti-slavery campaigners, journalists and the novelist Joseph Conrad. Travel writers may have helped to tempt the greedy abroad; travel writers also tried to build a swell of shame to send the greedy home again.

Of course, turning the tide of greed is much harder than providing temptation, even with today's more subtle forms of colonization. Today, the travel writer could write a book and copious articles about an overlooked paradise and open the floodgates to tourism, high-rise hotels, cultural distortion ... As the travel writer Simon Calder says, 'Benidorm begins with one back packer.' Although not all of us are perfect, there is an increased trend in modern travel writing to be self-conscious, humane and culturally aware. With the advent of fair trade, ecotourism and sustainable development has come a more philo-sophical type of writing, pondering the wrongs of the past and considering how many of the troubles in the world are the result of present-day selfish-ness, gluttony and carelessness on the part of wealthier countries. Perhaps in fifty years' time this kind of writing will be read with sadness because it was invariably ignored. Perhaps it will be rescued and shown to have, very slightly, very slowly, influenced a change in the way the world was run.

ON THE OUTSIDE BUT LOOKING IN

Largely ignored in the past were the writings of non-Europeans, who told of the history of colonialism and imperialism from their point of view. This was a sort of the opposite of travel writing – the arrived-upon describing the 'arrivers'. It still takes a trawl though specialist libraries and bookshops to find most of these accounts, by people native to a particular country, of their own history, but a modern travel writer could read them alongside the tales of European adventurers to get a fully rounded picture of a country's past.

And non-Europeans also wrote about the world beyond their own lands, although it was often not their choice to leave home. There were, for instance, non-European travel writers such as Olaudah Equiano who didn't choose to travel. Around 1755, he and his youngest sister were taken from West Africa to Barbados by slave traders. Then he was shipped to Virginia to be a house slave for a plantation owner. Equiano was subsequently sold to a British naval lieutenant and brought to London, he was sent to work on a warship and then sold to a merchant in Montserrat. Finally, he managed to buy his freedom and travelled the world as a ship's hairdresser. He went to Italy, Turkey, New York and Greenland. He returned to England where he became active in the abolitionist movement and wrote his memoirs. Much of his book, *The Interesting Narrative of the Life of Olaudah Equiano*, is a con-demnation of slavery. Alongside this, it shows the eighteenth-century world from a point of view much overlooked at the time, and less well remembered than works by his European contemporaries, travellers, factual writers and novelists, such as Sir Joseph Banks, Samuel Johnson and Jane Austen. Equiano's view of the world of their time is a startling reminder of how life was, if you happened to be born on the wrong continent:

> Our next voyage was to the Mediterranean. The ship was again got ready and we sailed in September for Genoa. This is one of the finest cities I ever saw; some of the edifices were of beautiful marble and made a most noble appearance, and many had very curious fountains before them. The churches were rich and magnificent and curiously adorned both in the inside and out. But all this

grandeur was, in my eyes, disgraced by the galley slaves whose condition, both there and in other parts of Italy, is truly piteous and wretched.

Olaudah Equiano, *The Interesting Narrative of the Life of Olaudah Equiano* (1789)

INTREPID WOMEN

Equiano's thought-provoking narrative of his life and travels came a few decades before the post-Napoleonic European travel craze known as 'The Grand Tour'. This period of avid travelling (perhaps there will be a name for our own one day – the grand backpack or the grand gap years?) was particularly interesting because it included a number of women among the travellers. To travel was suddenly seen as part of the education of a young lady – a wealthy young lady, that is. Unless she ran away to sea disguised as a man or sold her body around the ports, it was unusual for a woman not from a wealthy background to be travelling at this time. So the travellers' tales of this time do include women's writing but predominantly by women of means. There was so much of this travelling by ladies of means that Helen Sheridan, granddaughter of the playwright, wrote a spoof account of a lady's travels called *Lispings from Low Latitudes*, under the pen name 'The Hon. Impulsia Gushington'. It is a wonderful satire on the purple prose, melodrama and self-important foolishness committed to paper by voyaging ladies of means.

Lady Elisabeth Craven, like many of these wealthy ladies, travelled extensively in order to escape a dull marriage. She wrote long, gossipy memoirs and tended to travel in a liveried coach. Marguerite, Countess of Blessington wrote three travel narratives, referring to herself as 'The Idler' and did much to make Continental travel popular with ladies of quality. Also describing herself as 'idle' was Frances Elliot who wrote several irritated books about her travels in Europe, complaining about everything, including Rome, 'a third-rate modern city'. More admirable was Lady Jane Franklin, wife of the Arctic explorer Sir John Franklin. Franklin was lost in the Arctic and, largely at her own expense, Jane travelled the North Polar region for seven years to try to find out what happened to him. In the course of her search she gathered a vast amount of information about the region and was, in consequence, awarded the Royal Geographical Society's Gold Medal in 1860, the first woman to receive it. A little later came Isabella Bird, who travelled most of the world in an attitude she described as 'up to anything and freelegged'. Isabella was a tireless traveller and a prolific, if gushing, writer. Notorious for living with an outlaw in the Rocky Mountains, she carried on travelling after her paramour was shot dead and made one of her greatest journeys through China when she was in her sixties. She was also the first woman to address a meeting of the Royal Geographical Society in 1842.

Isabella would probably not have got on with Harriet Martineau, who, in 1838, wrote a stern volume called *How to Observe*, to instruct the serious traveller on what to look for abroad. Fun was never the point for Harriet, who became almost completely deaf in her forties but travelled with an ear trumpet to the Middle East: 'Egypt is not the country to go to for the recreation of travel. It is too suggestive and too confounding but to be met with in the spirit of study.'

Studious, speaking and reading Arabic, but with a little more sense of enjoyment in her travels was Gertrude Bell. She was one of the late nineteenth-century wave of women travellers, again women of means but generally a more highly educated group. Gertrude, always wearing the latest gown from Paris and usually having a full dinner service in her bags, was a remarkable traveller and scholar. She epitomizes the danger of travel writing – it can make history that, with hindsight, might better have been left unmade. She travelled Arabia's Empty Quarter and up through present-day Jordan, Syria and Iraq. She made archaeological discoveries, mapped uncharted territory and befriended tribal sheikhs whom she later helped to make rulers of new states. In a letter home in 1927, after helping to install Faisal ibn Husain as King of Iraq, she wrote, 'For, after all, to the best of our ability we were making history. But you may rely upon one thing – I'll never engage in making kings again; it's too great a strain ...'.

In those days, a European woman was treated as an honorary man. Bell took only passing glimpses at the lives of Arab women. When I travelled in the Jordanian desert I felt very feeble in comparison with Gertrude – I was meeting no sheikhs, making no maps, spoke just a smattering of Arabic and, among the Bedouin, I was relegated to the women's part of the tent. At first I felt a little sulky about the changed times I lived in – Gertrude Bell hadn't spent her time cleaning out goats' intestines and washing Bedouin children, a considerable part of my desert tent experience. Then I realized that I was seeing a side of life that previous great explorers of Arabia had not seen – the day-to-day life of the segregated women. I might never be Gertrude nor Lawrence of Arabia nor Wilfred Thesiger, but they had not lived the aspect of Bedouin life that I had. The world changes and travel writers find new subjects.

Not at the back of the tent doing housework, Gertrude made contacts and maps that served, among many soldiers and politicians of the time, Lawrence of Arabia well. After World War I she was a member of the Arab Intelligence Bureau in Cairo and played an influential part in the post-war carve-up of the Middle East by the British and the French authorities. In 1916 she set up residence in Baghdad as adviser to Faisal, the newly appointed King of Iraq, a role and a country that had not existed in these forms before European intervention. As the country and Faisal became more independent, Bell was marginalized. She spent her time setting up and managing the Museum of Baghdad. This extensive collection and its library were among the first things looted and destroyed after the fall of Saddam Hussein. The rise of this dictator, along with many current Middle Eastern troubles, can be traced clearly to the post-war, artificial creation of states in which Gertrude's writings and expertise were so important.

She died in Baghdad, probably of a deliberate overdose. She was ill, isolated from her own culture and increasingly excluded from any important role in the Middle East. Most of her busy travels were undertaken to escape the heart-break following an illicit and finally thwarted love affair.

Great travellers are often misfits in their society; a reassuring thought if you find yourself getting a little peculiar. But I do not think being a mis-fit is a prerequisite, it can be just as useful to understand your own society, the society you will be taking your writing back to, as it is to understand another culture.

Although very much a loner, Gertrude Bell was of her time. She carried with her many of the cultural assumptions of her era and, despite a rebellious spirit, could not leap out of the society she came from completely. This happens, inevitably, to all writers. We can't see into the future to see whether our viewpoint will be contradicted by the facts; we can't foretell how social rules will change. It is possible, though, for us to be aware that our culture and the attitudes of our time may not be the best.

The travel writer may be, like any writer, a somewhat eccentric and isolated figure, but part of the evolution of the form does seem to involve an increased level of political and cultural awareness. Even the most influ-ential and expert of today's travel writers tend to steer clear of the machina-tions of governments and would be wary of 'making kings'. The travel writer has become more independent and far more thoughtful about the possible consequences of their actions. The days when misfits and adventurers could regard the rest of the world as a playground are still with us in a different form. Rogue traders and mercenaries people the less known parts of the world today. Travel writers are more likely to expand on or back up reports from journalists concerned with the cruelty and exploitation still rife around the globe. Travel writers may have less fun than they used to but they probably try to be more useful.

WOMEN TRAVELLERS TODAY

Women travellers are now from a much wider cross-section of life. Some travel for adventure – Polly Evans, Josie Dew, Sarah Wheeler and Dervla Murphy, to name a handful; while others, like Jane Goodall or Lynn Cox, travel and live abroad because they are following a passion. In Jane Goodall's case, a passion for studying and protecting the chimpanzee; Lynn Cox travels to break long-distance swimming records in extraordinary environments. With all these women, their writings reflect their very different takes on life.

Women are slowly catching up in the field of travel writing, but the lack of non-European viewpoints is still more significant in its dearth. As for the lack of non-European female viewpoints ... In her book *My Travels around the World*, the Egyptian doctor and writer Nawal el Saadawi shows how travel for women from certain cultures, regardless of their wealth or education, is not always a simple matter. Nawal Al Saadawi is at Cairo airport, about to catch a flight to a medical conference. A policeman looks through all her papers and wants to know, in addition to her permissions from the state, where is the permission to travel she should have obtained from her husband? The law in Egypt at that time didn't allow married women to travel unaccompanied with out proof of their husband's consent. Nawal Al Saadawi is lucky; she has brought her divorce certificate to the airport with her. The policeman still examines this carefully to be sure it is authentic but finally he accepts that Al Saadawi is a free woman, with the right to travel unaccompanied.

Although the history of travel writing has included some remarkable women, and their numbers have increased, it is still unusual to find women who make a point of being a female observer of the world. Women writers tend to be serious and determined to show that they can do anything the men can do, or more. I think there are new routes for women to follow. Being exceptional and physically courageous can help, but so can being curious and observant of the more mundane details of people's lives. All over the world there are more people doing housework than are having adventures – so there is a case for the female travel writer to forget competing with the mountain leaping men. Not only does being female allow access to previously unexplored sides of life, previously unconsidered aspects of people's lives could be written about.

Some may find these irritating and controversial thoughts, but I think that it is important to point out that there are ways to be a travel writer that don't involve leading a camel train through a desert. Travellers such as Gertrude Bell had a very high status, but adopting a low status, blending in, can give a writer a very good vantage point. There is still a great deal of the world where women are invisible, not considered – disappearing among them could be fascinating. In this post-colonial world being a female traveller also has many advantages in parts of the world where history means that white men are seen as a threat, even if they are the most agreeable, gentle and well-intentioned of male travellers.

NEW ATTITUDES, NEW CONCERNS

There are still few travel books written by overtly gay men or women. As times have changed in some parts of the world, this could be a new point of view to explore. How do gay travellers survive homophobic countries? How liberal are supposedly liberal countries? In what different ways do different societies accommodate sexuality? Are there ancient cultures where sexuality is seen as a gift of the gods and nothing to make a fuss about?

Mainly for financial reasons but also because of the lack of widespread education, many writers of the past were from privileged backgrounds. Cheap flights, together with a more democratic attitude to travel and education, mean that there's a new tone of voice in some travel books. They're written by people who don't feel they were born to command, who have no explorer ancestors and who have to watch their spending carefully. There are new travel books concerned with the things that worry ordinary travellers – not how to manage the unruly bearers, but how to wrestle a backpack onto a crowded bus; not the nuisance of shipping out decent claret, but the nuisance of needing to save the bus fare to get home from the airport.

Who the traveller is when they set out can influence the type of book they write to the extent that they can explore previously uncharted cultural territory.

All the time, the horizons shift for travel writers. There are stories still to tell. Concerns for the environment and wildlife leads many writers on their travels. A master at making his point while telling his story is the affable and much bearded writer Tim Cahill. In *Pecked to Death by Ducks* Cahill is passionate about the endangered mountain gorillas of Rwanda. Skilfully, he involves us with the gorillas, tells us their names and presents them as characters to the reader, before telling us the bad news. He proceeds to describe the many ways the modern world has found to destroy the creatures, from hunting them to cutting down the forests they live in.

Cahill often reports on efforts to protect wildlife and investigates instances where species are being exploited or destroyed. This takes him to far-flung places, where he meets extraordinary characters. He has all the usual material of travelogues in his work, but his interest in conservation and protection of species is a distinctly modern thread running through it.

In general, a more thoughtful approach to the survival of wildlife has emerged in travel writing, as has a widespread concern for the environment. Travel writers no longer worry so much about how to get where they are going, but whether they should go at all. In 1993, the traveller Simon Calder wrote in *The Independent*:

> The destinations which the eco-tourist should steer towards fall into two categories. The first comprises places where tourism is being developed in a thoughtful way, such as Belize in Central America or the Seychelles in the Indian Ocean. The second is less seductive: if you are serious about being sensitive, you should go to Benidorm or some other place where you cannot make much difference to the existing mess.

Calder now writes a regular column describing his adventures as a hitch hiker and cyclist – activities he undertakes to offset the carbon footprint he creates with frequent flying. There is so much for the modern travel writer to worry about that avoiding being eaten by bears might be the easy part. But if the ethics of going anywhere at all are part of what the writer sees as the problem, then that is a new layer to go into the work. The travel writer doesn't always have to campaign direct. As always, it depends on the character and the style of the writer. Books like Tony Hawks's *Playing the Moldovans at Tennis* gives a light-hearted, individualizing insight into a people who might previously have been seen as very other, a mysterious mass from a depressing post-Soviet land over there somewhere behind Europe.

OTHER NEW THEMES

There are many ways for a travel writer to bring the troubles of the world to life and to accentuate detail from a big canvas. In her lyrical book *Mali Blues*, Lieve Joris travels with a Malian musician, noting how frustratingly hard his life is. The book obliquely provokes many questions about the way African talent is underestimated or exploited by the European music industry. In our lives we seem to have a constant stream of new worries, but at least they can provide new, insightful strands to travel writing.

Another new worry for travel writers is that they now live in an age where they can be caught in a lie. If they are not followed by tourists to a destination, there will invariably be a good documentary on the area available to the armchair traveller, as well as dozens of informative internet sites. The travel writer has to ponder more carefully why their insight into a place would be interesting, valuable or entertaining, just to go where most people do not go is not enough. And, most difficult of all, writing about a place where people flock for their holidays takes real ingenuity. Yet this can be simply a matter of being involved in a community abroad in a way the average, hurried traveller might not be.

In *Driving over Lemons*, Chris Stewart describes setting up home in Andalucia. Planeloads of Brits charge through it every year and there are thousands who have made their home there. But Stewart has advantages: he can speak good Spanish and he can shear sheep. These skills involve him with the locals far more successfully than the '*Uno Sangria por favor*' level of the rest of us. He also takes a wife on his adventure; she has to have a baby and rear this baby in a remote sheep farm – not everyone's experience. Stewart's book is about a very familiar destination; he is merely setting up home abroad, not sailing iceberg-filled, uncharted waters – but he is still doing something many of us only think about. Or he is doing something large numbers of people have done, but his book provides a chance to compare and contrast experiences. He is that amiable companion on the journey to live abroad, or a useful aversion therapy for those considering a similar venture.

Stewart's book sold widely, as have other, similar 'going to live abroad' books. A few years ago, comedy was the fashion in travel writing best sellers. Now the accounts of moving abroad are selling best. In a few years' time a new fashion may emerge, but each wave of travel writing means that the travel writer has to battle a little harder to stand out. Early travel writers just had to get there and string a halfway coherent report together. Now they have to prove they are funnier, smarter, more observant, more involved, more articulate ... But there is less danger from bears.

Stewart's success relied on his language and practical skills as well as his affable writing persona. These are all subtle things to set a travel writer apart and make him or her a best seller. Spotting one's subtle advantages and unique skills for oneself is certainly as difficult as, if very different from, the difficulties involved in the life of a Victorian making a reckless dash to find the source of the Nile.

The Rise of the Tourist

No writer was more biting against what he considered the tide of vulgarity crowding through Europe than Thackeray: 'Times are altered at Ostend now; of the Britons who go thither, very few look like lords, or act like members of our hereditary aristocracy. They seem for the most part shabby in attire, dingy of linen, lovers of billiards and brandy, and cigars and greasy ordinaries.'

Alan Sillitoe, *Leading the Blind: A Century of Guidebook Travel 1815–1911*

Modern travel writers have more to think about, more competition and libraries full of prior knowledge to contend with, but just as painting and sculpture shifted to accommodate the arrival of photography, travel writing has become a more subtly complex form, and also a richer, more diverse and thought-provoking form. Although humour abounds, it is a more serious form than it once was. In a marketplace where there are checks and balances provided by documentaries, readers' own travel experiences, journalism and cultural awareness and cultural diversity among the writers of books, the careless adventuring recorded in the travel books of yesteryear looks like the more shallow, simplistic and underdeveloped version of the form. All this being said, what readers love to find in travel writing is a reason to smile. If a travel writer can tell a funny story and that offends no one, then they can be excused concerns with ecology, the balance of power and the wrongs of history. The world has been and always will be a pretty silly place. How travel writers use humour has undoubtedly changed, along with the determination among comedians not to offend genders, races or creeds for a cheap laugh. When laughs aren't cheap, they're harder to come by. But they are still out there to find.

There is a change in the tone, style and content of modern travel writing. These days, travel writers have to think harder, research further and make an attempt to understand what they see abroad. Or, at least, in the case of the more light-hearted and anecdotal travel writers explain that the reasons they don't understand what they see are entirely the result of their own shortcomings. Destinations may also change – there is a big universe out there. In a few hundred years the adventurous could scatter into the galaxies – some sensible, some silly, writing up their travels for the folks back home on earth. Travel writing will once again be about new frontiers, completely uncharted territory. Hopefully the new era of exploration will be an ethical one. Let's hope, for those of us on the silly edge of the travel-writing market, that we do one day get to avoid long-haul flights and just have to say; 'Beam me up!'

FINDING YOUR STYLE

WHO ARE YOU?

What type of travel writer you are really depends on what type of person you are. There is no point trying to write a comical book if you are a sensitive, studious type. There is no point pretending to knowledge you don't have and there is no need to cycle the Gobi desert if you like to hang around in bars, smoking and swapping jokes.

To a large extent, who you are when you are not writing should determine your travel writing style. In fiction, writers can imagine themselves to be of another gender, race, age – they can even be from another planet; but in travel writing, although imaginative skills are required, the closer to yourself you write, the more alive the book will be. Of course, it does take imagination to understand another culture, to empathize with people encountered along the way and to want to travel in the first place, but to pretend to be someone else in a travel book is seldom sustainable.

When writing scripts, I was commissioned to write a film starring the comedian Lenny Henry. The film was set in Ireland and I tried to drive around the Sligo countryside, imagining how it would feel to be making the journey as a six-foot Jamaican man. The exercise gave me some interesting thoughts and insights, but, when I did eventually write a book about travelling around Ireland, I wrote as myself.

Personal connections and passions led me on the journey that became my Irish travel book, but the book includes other things too. A few years on, if I glance back through this book, I can see the moments where I lost interest, where I was describing something I felt I ought to be interested in because it was of historical importance, but actually some trivial thing beside it was what really caught my attention. Or a conversation held outside the famous monument stuck in my mind far more vividly than the monument itself. I came across a leading political figure and was fascinated by his choice of suit, not cross-examining him about power-sharing initiatives in Northern Ireland. The trivial, the conversation and the suit were the stuff of travel writing – the stuff of my style of writing anyway. The rest I could have left for the guide-book writers, historians and journalists to deal with more expertly.

Writers seldom know what their style is to begin with. They discover it and hone it as they go along. Just as a person has long-standing interests and passions but will discover other interests and fascinations as they go through life. Style, like character, is not fixed solidly at an early age.

As I spend half my writing life as a dramatist and began as a dramatist, conversations are important to me and I remember them easily. Physical descriptions and facts I need to note down quickly, because they don't lodge firmly in my head. And I have to force myself even to notice them. I particularly like conversations with a bit of drama – an argument, an eavesdropping that breaks my heart, a comical piece of wheeler dealing ... My knowledge of politics, history, architecture, art and science is cursory, so it is always the human detail that dominates in what I write. Having also been a joke writer, I do tend to tour the world in search of comedy. All this is neither correct nor incorrect, it is simply part of a style I have developed. Am developing; if I thought that I wasn't going to get any better what would be the point?

Writing, like the travelling itself, is a journey. There are destinations reached and books completed but there is no real ending. I haven't been to a tenth of the places I want to go to, I haven't written a book that doesn't irritate me for its feebleness and flaws a few weeks after completion. Next time I shall do better. Next time as a writer I hope that I'll find a better vocabulary, more economical descriptions, more concise opinions and a broader range of references. I hope that I will not always settle for the parts of writing that come easily, but develop new skills. I also hope that I shall become a more empathic, witty, astute, honest, courageous, well-informed and imaginative person, thus making me an improved writer. There's no harm in trying.

There are athletic travel writers, erudite travel writers, journalistic writers and writers more inclined to revel in the natural world. Their success or failure depends on how closely these writing interests reflect their interests as people. This does not mean that a writer has to be completely obsessive and narrow-minded as they collect material. An athletic adventurer can have a poetic moment and the nature lover could suddenly be distracted by a local political intrigue. Writers learn their strengths and their primary characteristics, but it is possible to remain truthful while improving the areas of weakness. For me, it is always to find a way to use physical description that doesn't read as though another writer had popped in to write a few sentences for me.

WAYS TO DEVELOP A STYLE

When planning a journey that you hope will become a book, there will be a central interest that you will want to follow. After deciding on your primary interest, there are secondary ones to consider too. Are you interested in the process of travel? Culture? Dialogue? Architecture? Costume? Food? Flora and fauna? When you notice that you are not very interested in scenery or food, it is probably best not to write about them, or you could just be making lists – but be prepared for something to surprise you. Keep observing and thinking outside your primary interest in case you discover a new layer of yourself. There may be struggle then, to write about something that wouldn't usually catch your attention, but there may be ways to make writing about these things come alive and fit your style. Make lists, just for yourself, of things you would not normally consider on a journey. A simple bus ride is a good place for the experiment: I would immediately be hoping for conversations to eavesdrop on, but to stretch myself I would try to describe the bus, the passengers' clothes and faces, the passing scenery and the architecture of the towns. I would think about how the journey makes me feel and possibly look into the bus route – why does it go the way it does, who uses it and why? I may end up with some very dull pages I shall discard, but there could be some unexpected gem to set among the usual material I would record about a journey. If the unexpected observation genuinely caught my interest, it shouldn't be too difficult to write about it in a way that fits with my usual way of writing. Not too difficult.

All the same, for a writer, finding their style can be as difficult as that dreadful advice uttered to people when they feel shy, to 'just be yourself', thus immediately provoking an identity crisis and making the anxiety far worse. It is the sort of advice that used to send me demented as a timid teenager – I'd end up wanting to lock myself in the wardrobe and never go out until I could disguise myself as someone else, anyone else. In writing, things are easier than they are in life. You don't have to walk into that party full of strangers. It is all on paper. You can be witty, charming, observant ... All the things you would really be in public, if you were not too scared to open your mouth in a crowded room.

Does this contradict what I'm saying about writing as yourself? I don't believe that it does. Many writers have a different self on paper from the person one might meet in the supermarket. My writing style is chatty, but in person you would have to get to know me quite well before I chatted as freely as I do on paper. Some writers describe themselves as having a writing persona. I suggest that it is an edited self. And often a hidden self, an inner self – the self reserved for your closest friends.

You may be a very chatty person in the supermarket. In that case your writing persona might have to tone down the chat. Edit the cheery flow of words to the essentials, creating moments to pause and reflect. I am more fearful, irritable and absent-minded in reality than I am on paper. I include these character flaws in my books, but not too much. I am not hiding anything – I just pick the moments where my anxiety is particularly ridiculous, my irritability particularly unreasonable and my scattiness has resulted in disaster. Every instance of my being a flawed and feeble character would be boring and repetitive. I use key examples of my shortcomings to give the impression of who I am. Some writers choose to keep themselves out of the story. There will be a lot less use of 'I' in their writing than in my books. This doesn't mean they are not there, they are just quieter about it.

Jan Morris comes to mind as a writer whose sensitive and humorous character seeps through the understated prose of her journeys. An elegant example of her style is the short book *A Sultan in Oman*, published in 1957. Not all of us will have the chance of a journey like this one – being invited to travel across remote country with the Sultan of Oman as he consolidates his newly formed kingdom, but it is Morris' writing as much as the journey itself that make this a remarkable book. It is packed with humour, history, anthropology, literary reference, stunning description and astute political commentary. A typical page moves from humour, to suspense, to melancholy to evocative description. There is individual action, then stillness, then a crowd movement, then stillness again. There is general history, then personal observation, then a return to an overview.

Morris writes with the control of a good film director. There are crowd scenes, close-ups; action and reflective scenes. This is probably subconscious in a writer as experienced yet instinctive as Morris, but it is a good technique to remember: think of the incident you want to describe as if it were a series of scenes in a film you're directing. What are the principal characters doing and saying? Where are the extras and what do we need them for? Is the landscape important to punctuate the scene? Has the scene gone on too long or been cut too sharply? Would a sharp cut convey the mood effectively? Or do you need a slow dissolve into the next moment?

Thinking of sentences as camera shots in a film is a useful technique if you feel stuck for a way to write a scene. It can help to break down a complicated incident into manageable moments. What do you want the reader to be looking at? When do you want their gaze to shift? When do you want their feelings to change? Techniques are the tools you use to build your style. Some writers seem to be born with a facility to use these tools; the rest of us have to keep practising until we are good with the tools and until we know which ones suit us better than others. Finding a style, or finding your own voice, means finding the delicate balance between being honest and avoiding self-indulgence. It is the balance between attempting self-improvement and avoiding strain in reaching for the unattainable.

LEARNING FROM EXPERIENCE

I know that I shall never cycle anywhere, hike anywhere or climb anywhere high. I have no interest in places where nature is abundant and the animals will be my friend. I also have no interest in crossing Arctic wastes where there's nothing for days but snow and white bears. Physical exertion, pitting myself against the elements, going places where there are no people to meet and there is no human culture to observe have no allure for me. This still leaves a lot to do. So perhaps that is a start to defining your style – make a list of what you definitely don't want to do, see or take an interest in.

The book of mine I dislike the most, *The Winner's Enclosure*, about travelling around Australia, suffers because I just did not like the place. It was too empty, there was too much sport to do and not enough interaction with people who interested me. The sections of the book that come alive are where I meet people I like – there is talk, there are stories, there are thoughts shared, there is communication. Through the rest of the book my boredom is tangible. Encountering people I dislike and satirizing them becomes repetitious. One reviewer called me an 'unabashed whingeing pom' – he was correct. And a whinger does become tiresome on a journey. The mistakes in this book were invaluable though, I knew from then on that the maps of my journeys were to be about meetings with people who intrigued me, not ticking off sights and destinations on a map. I realized that I was not good at describing scenery, analysing politics or enthusing about barbecues. I knew that I was not one of those satirical writers who can manage successfully to sustain a whole book complaining about a place they cannot get to grips with.

The next book I wrote, *Show Me the Magic*, was about 200 pages too long in its original form. I had far too much of a good time, was too fascinated and crazed to tell everything that had happened to me in West Africa. And far too much had happened. Luckily, a good editor with an endless supply of pencils showed me how to recognize where I was telling the same kind of anecdote twice, giving three different stories to illustrate the same point and forgetting that it was not necessarily my job to tell everyone absolutely everything about West Africa in one book.

So, knowing yourself and editing yourself are an essential part of style. The reader wants to hear your voice, but not too much of it. Make your point once and move on, unless you are sure you really need repetition to emphasize your enthusiasm, bile, outrage or confusion. The reader can also hear your voice going flat when you are not very interested in your destination and your descriptions are desultory. If you don't watch out for them, the reader will notice your verbal ticks and become irritated by them. Beginning a sentence with 'So' is definitely one of mine.

There are several ways by which to keep a stern eye on yourself. Once you have finished a piece, leave it for at least a week. Then print it out and read it on paper. If you write it in longhand, type it and then read it. Seeing it in a different form will shake up your perception. Reading the piece aloud to yourself is a useful way to hear where the tone sounds forced or to hear sentences that are clumsy. This is also a good way to spot your favourite, much overused words. Running the 'find' facility on a computer is another way to check on yourself, if you suspect that you are overusing a word or phrase.

Looking at your words once you have written them down is the only way to start getting a sense of your own style. Are you brusque and to the point? Are you a meandering poetic writer? Are the words you favour romantic or matter-of-fact? Are you careful and formal, or slangy and conversational? Again, none of these are right or wrong; they are simply things to consider when discovering the writing style that suits you.

TRICKS OF THE TRADE

Most people when they're starting out as travel writers keep a diary. This is essential, but a more useful way to develop a style for public consumption is to write an account of your travels as if it were a letter to a friend, a smart, curious but easily bored friend. Imagine that all you have is one of those air letter forms, so the account will have to be brief. You don't want your friend to think you are tedious; you don't want them to miss the funniest, most moving or thought-provoking moment of your experience. Whenever I feel stuck about how to describe an incident, I imagine that I am writing for my friend – this loosens me up, enabling me to be myself. And as the friend I have in mind is a lawyer who likes to laugh, I have to be sharp, funny and not leave any loose ends that could be used against me in cross-examination. But sometimes, if no amount of trying can make an incident or scene come alive, it can be useful to remember the phrase, 'I guess you had to be there'. There are moments and places that 'words can't adequately describe' – a phrase that no writer worth the ink should ever use. If a thousand attempts cannot find the words, don't make excuses for yourself, just don't tell the story. Perhaps, the story will come back to you a few years on, when your skills and insights are more developed and the way to tell it, or the true significance of it, will occur to you. The small exercise of writing letters is part of the only real way to develop your style, and that is to write and write. All the time imagining that what you are writing is not private, someone else has to understand it, believe it and be intrigued by it.

It constantly surprises me how many people travel widely and want to write about it but don't read travel writing. Reading history, novels, guide books and journalism is important, but not to read good travel writing is a strange handicap to give oneself. How else would you know what is a travel writing cliché? How would you know from experience why good travel writing stands out?

Although I am not very interested in nature, mountaineering, snow with bears or Australia, I would be happy to read travellers on those subjects, if the writing was good enough. I would feel I had enjoyed an armchair experience, learning about something I had no interest in doing myself.

Sometimes travel writers assume a readership among fellow enthusiasts. The mark of a really good travel book is that it is interesting to the person who is not really interested. No one likes to sit for hours in a bar listening to someone else talk about their sailing holiday, hiking trip or camping tour, unless the talker is a great storyteller – or the listener is particularly fascinated by yachts, hiking routes or camp sites. If the pub bore had a companion eaten by seagulls, wolves or bears then possibly he might get away with poor story-telling skills. But good style is all about making a story where nothing astounding happens into readable material, or about communicating an enthusiasm in a way that doesn't drive those who do not share the enthusiasm screaming for the door.

A mistake I have come across while tutoring travel writing courses is that students have been on life-changing journeys to amazing places and they think that that will carry their writing through. As an exercise to annoy these students, I ask them to write a piece describing a journey that takes them from their home to the supermarket and back that has to fascinate and amuse me. Then, to annoy them more, I ask them to write about an imaginary country that can be as bizarre as they like, but again, it has to fascinate and entertain. The purpose of these exercises is to take away their props. They are left thinking about the writing and not leaning on the wonders of their travel experiences to draw the reader in. Looking at a mundane place, thinking hard about it, can be oddly revealing. Perhaps not as life-changing as a camel trek to Timbuktu, but an interesting way to flex the writing muscles.

Although one would imagine that the broadcaster Mark Lawson would have enough to do without writing travel books, he did write a very entertaining account of his journeys to places he described as 'activity challenged' or 'differently interesting'. The book was called, *The Battle for Room Service: Journeys to All the Safe Places.* He went to Canada, Switzerland, Belgium, New Zealand and even managed to make Milton Keynes intriguing. He didn't make me want to go to Milton Keynes, but he did hold my interest in reading about it: Why does Milton Keynes feel so soulless? Lawson suggests that it is because the new town focuses on the car rather than the human being. Milton Keynes seems deserted and somewhat sinister because most people are moving around in vehicles. This is not the type of urban living we are used to in Britain and it is particularly disconcerting to see street signs around the mall in Milton Keynes that read 'Pedestrians do not have priority'.

Lawson manages to involve us in a dull place by looking for the human detail, and finding its absence is the key to the atmosphere of his destination. Discovering ways to describe soulless ugliness can be as challenging as describing beauty in an original way. Taking the general perception of a place and contradicting it, or supporting and analysing it, can be a useful way to mull over the impression a destination creates. Lawson also performs a useful service in saving us all the trouble of having to go to Milton Keynes for ourselves. Imagining that you are writing about a destination the reader will probably never visit is a good way to concentrate the mind on making your description vivid and full – as good as a visit. The journeys we shall never make may be the ones we enjoy reading about the most.

I am afraid of falling into water and so would be very unlikely to make a sea voyage in anything other than an enormous, steady, ocean liner that is going nowhere near icebergs, but reading Johnathan Raban on the sea or boats is such a pleasure that I don't feel that I am missing out. In his essay *Sea Room* he describes a restless summer where he has a recurring daydream of a man alone in a boat at sea, a boat that is really more like 'an ark'. Raban keeps imagining this carefree man, heading across the sea in his boat, laughing at those left behind to worry about work, mortgages and the concerns of the land.

For those with no desire to run away to sea, this piece still draws us in. We all have some fantasy of escape, even if it is not quite this, and so the fancy has broad appeal. Raban then builds a picture of why he wants to escape and describes how it feels to finally do so. The sea-going is almost irrelevant – the story is about restlessness, discontent and a longing to recreate oneself. It is a rare person who has not had one of those feelings, so the writing draws in even the most feeble of landlubbers. While, at the same time, there are rich seams of information about boats and going to sea. Landlubbers learn something while sailors can delight in recognition.

In *Worlds Apart* Gavin Young meets with the legendry explorer Wilfred Thesiger at his home in Africa. Thesiger tells Young that, in all his remarkable journeys through Africa and Arabia, it has always been the people that interested him. And in his experiences, having seen great landscapes and shocking events, Thesiger knows the key to good storytelling is finding a small nugget of an anecdote in a mountain of experience, and tells Young about Orde Wingate, a commander in Britain's East African campaigns in what was then Abyssinia. He reveals the extraordinary memory that Orde Wingate would lie in his tent stark naked, smoothing his pubic hair with someone else's toothbrush. This wasn't a secret, because it was what Wingate did whilst giving orders to his officers. Stunned, Gavin Young asks how Thesiger knew it was someone else's toothbrush? Thesiger gives another wry insight into Wingate's eccentric character by saying that he doubted Wingate had a toothbrush of his own.

In reading Thesiger's journeys through remote places, it is his attachment to human detail that makes his writing as characterful as his journeys were remarkable. If he were writing to a friend from the middle of the Abyssinian campaign, it would surely be the vivid and bizarre toothbrush story he would tell first. Then, having caught the attention, he might describe the rest of the Abyssinia campaign, if he thought it was an interesting yarn. Let war reporters do the reporting and historians the analysing – the toothbrush belongs to the travel writer. Matching the physical rigours of Thesiger's journeys might not be possible for most of us. However, elements of his writing style, such as making vastness manageable by starting with a striking, human detail, that is the sort of thing any writer could emulate.

Finding your style in travel writing is first of all about making the kind of journey that interests you. It may be physically challenging or a journey in search of spiritual enlightenment. It could be about finding a lost past, or simply looking for laughs. If the journey sits comfortably and honestly with you as a person, then the second part of finding your style will not be as difficult as it might be. The second part is learning how to tell your story to someone who is not as interested in you or your subject as you are. The trick of it is, I think, to cross Mongolia on a yak, or whatever it is takes your fancy, but always to write about it as if you were trying to make a dull place come alive. But don't expect Mongolia, or the yak, to be enough. We can see Mongolia and yaks galore on the Discovery Channel. Make us see the detail they have missed and hear the people they didn't interview. Make your particular experience in Mongolia have a universal resonance. And, most of all, tell us a story.

Be bold, make mistakes and try different ways of telling your story. Write it, rather than think about it. Pondering the words for too long can be like singing in the bath – a very different matter from singing in public. Getting the words out of your head and on to paper, or screen, is the first step to going public. The words, then the sentences have to be there in front of you to be looked at. You may look at them and hurl them into the waste basket – but you didn't *know* they were wrong until you tried them out. Nobody knows how they write until they've written. And written, and then written some more.

WHERE ARE YOU GOING AND WHY?

THE KICK-OFF

It is important to make a good start. A sharp, sparse statement can draw the eye and interest the reader in continuing. They may continue because they agree or because they disagree – it doesn't matter. The thing is to engage their interest – and quickly. Even the sort of words in this kind of opening can matter – are they definite, simple, unqualified? They should demand support from the sentence that follows, luring the reader in.

Without a forceful start you are beginning to lose the reader before the first page is finished. The book may become fascinating, but what if the reader never gets to page 50 to find that companions-eaten-by-bears moment that you describe so well? As they say on film-writing courses, 'start in the middle of the movie.' Plunge the reader into the action, so they feel eager to read on and catch up.

> I'm thinking I might actually enjoy this, if I had more time.
>
> It's Sunday, the first day of the week: the one that's for resting and possibly talking to God, but I am doing neither. I am sitting across my window ledge and thinking that Sundays are always much the same: vaguely peaceful and emptied and smug: and I am looking out over my gutter and four storeys down to my street. It's late in a mild afternoon and there are flickers of spring in the trees. The smell of young grass drifts up to me from the park and the air is also coloured very slightly with waking earth and sunny masonry. Cars beetle past, roofs gleaming, but there's no one out walking. Although I'd expect there might be on such a pleasant day, there is no one about.
>
> Which means I should do this. I should jump now, while I can.
>
> A.L. Kennedy, *On Bullfighting* (Yellow Jersey Press, 1999)

The action can be personal, introspective, or it can be the rush of people involved in the start of a journey:

> We made a great stir in Antwerp docks. A stevedore and a lot of dock porters took up the two canoes, and ran with them for the slip. A crowd of children followed

cheering. The *Cigarette* went off in a splash and a bubble of small breaking water. Next moment the *Arethusa* was after her. A steamer was coming down, men on the paddle-box shouted hoarse warnings, the stevedore and his porters were bawling from the quay. But in a stroke or two the canoes were away and out in the middle of the Scheldt, and all steamers and stevedores, and other longshore vanities were left behind.

R.L. Stevenson, An Inland Voyage (1878)

Another active and involving way to begin is with a conversation. Perhaps a conversation about something that epitomizes the type of place the writer is in and the company he or she is keeping, as well as suggesting the type of person the writer is. In *Show Me the Magic*, the thriller-like politics in the obscure West African state of Benin was one of the things that first attracted me to the country. I wanted to get this information in early in the book so readers unfamiliar with the country would know that Benin was an exciting place. The conversation actually happened quite a while into the journey, but I saw it as a useful way to explain the fascination of the country and to introduce the bizarre relationship between my bewildered self and my guide and driver Isidore, that was to be a vital component in the book.

'This where the politician exploded.' Isidore waved a hand at the town sign. 'Paf! And gone.'

I thought he was talking about a bomb.

Benin had violently changed governments nine times in twelve years during the nervy, bad old days between 1960 and 1972. One political hopeful declared himself president at nine in the morning and was gone by teatime. Running Benin was no job for anyone looking for a good night's sleep, a pension plan or a long life – until President Kerekou came along in 1972 and showed how a tough guy with a heavily scarred face, and no qualms about house smashings or random arrests, could keep himself in charge for a very long time. Yet even under Kerekou's stern regime, coup enthusiasts made sure no more than three years passed without running, shouting, shooting and bleeding outside the presidential palace, right up until the late nineties. So when I heard talk of exploded politicians, a bomb did seem likely.

'Who blew him up?' Isidore looked at me, then quickly back at the road – in these country towns a chicken or a child could be darting recklessly in front of the car at any moment. 'In fact', he said. 'He did it himself.'

'An accident?'

Regardless of small darting perils on the road, Isidore had to look at me again. As always, impatience was tempered to a long-suffering weariness, the way the good-natured remind themselves not to snap at the slow-witted – just take a deep breath and try to communicate, yet again.

'How could it be an accident? You know the story?'

'No.'

'No. So how can you talk of an accident when you're hearing this for the first time?'

I said nothing. Isidore drove on a while, composing his thoughts for the storytelling, steeling himself to deal with further treacle-headed incomprehension, bound to spoil things before his punchline if he didn't keep strict control of the conversation.

Annie Caulfield, *Show Me the Magic* (Viking Penguin, 2002)

Starting in a conversation hooks readers in to your story and works as a beginning if readers are quite quickly reassured that all will be explained by your providing some background or context for the initial conversation. At the start of *Trawler*, Redmond O'Hanlan uses a raucous telephone call to intrigue us, to let us know this will be an action-packed book – and then explains what this frantic telephone call was all about. There's talk of storms, there's use of fishing terms and gales blowing ... although the call is hard to understand, we understand enough to sense the world we're entering will probably be dangerous as well as exciting. O'Hanlan is given instructions to meet the caller early in the morning, so this is both an opening with a conversation and an active beginning. We know O'Hanlan has a short time to put his affairs in order, before he has to be off into the storms and gales blowing.

A letter, telegram or phone call are all devices I've seen used at the start of a travel book. Presumably these days there would also be emails and texts. This is another category of opening gambit – a summons. It could be urgent, fascinating or perhaps at first resisted by the author. There is a problem to be solved, an adventure in the offing, an opportunity opening up, or a long-lost friend turning out to be breeding alpacas in the Andes and in need of a hand. The summons is like the treasure map found at the beginning of old stories. The author might be wary of high seas and pirates ahead but we know they will go eventually. A summons could lure the author on to a quest, which is a great structural device for a travel book.

SOME DAY I'LL FIND YOU

A sure fire way to draw the reader in is to set out on a quest, involving them quickly in the piece of detective work you'll be undertaking. For example, Gavin Young's book *In Search of Conrad* is fairly self-explanatory before it is even opened. Where did the writer work, live, get his inspiration and what record is there of him in far-flung places? The places themselves are fascinating and Conrad has a wide following of people who would be attracted to a book like this. The adventure has begun in the book's title.

A man with an even wider following, Father Christmas, is the subject of Jeremy Seal's quest in *Santa – A Life*. Again this is fairly self-explanatory. Seal uses his extensive historical and geographical knowledge of Turkey to trace the origins of the real Santa, Saint Nicholas, and then follows the saint's journey to world domination. The detective work is given a personal drive because Seal has small children; for their sake, he wants to find out all there is to know about Santa Claus, beyond the tawdry manifestations in Christmas shopping malls. Remembering his own lost love of Santa Claus is something Seal adds in to the quest to draw reading adults along with him. Yes, we all remember finding out that Santa wasn't real, but here's a book promising to show us that he is real after all – sort of. Hard to resist.

Sometimes a good beginning is to present an interesting, possibly provocative theory. It will be clear that your book will go on to expand on this. This is particularly useful if you intend to write about somewhere well-known but from a different angle. Andy Soutter has a challenging subtitle to his book *Australiaville: Souvenirs of Post-Civilization*. Clearly this is going to be something more than cricket and kangaroos. His first paragraph immediately elaborates the controversial subtitle, claiming that one of Australia's great contributions to the modern world is the suburb. As most outsiders think of the Sydney Opera house or the wide open Outback as typically Australian, the beginning of the book draws us in by upsetting our expectations.

The best motives for journeys are often personal ones that spread out to include the interests of many people. In *The European Tribe*, Caryl Phillips wants to look at his own place in Europe and the place in Europe of other Afro-Caribbean people by travelling among and examining Europeans. He begins with the chastening realization that will send him on his journey. As a young man he goes to the United States and realizes for the first time that it is possible for a black person to have a career as a writer. In Britain this had never occurred to him. In his school he had never been shown a text that was written by a black person, or concerned itself with black people's lives. His childhood was in 1970s Britain, where the sense of a distinct social identity for black citizens hadn't been formed – or was discouraged where it began to form.

He goes on to relate childhood examples of racism he encountered in Britain and quickly establishes that his particular version of the Grand Tour will be a real eye-opener. Phillips was brought up in Europe but travels through it feeling an outsider, and is often perceived as an outsider. The book promises a refreshing and educative point of view for the white European reader, unused to being the observed in modern travel writing; and the black reader is promised an unusual opportunity to be the observer. There is discovery and recognition in the story.

In *Looking for George*, Helena Drysdale rapidly engages the reader in her quest to find a lost person from her past.

> Each of us was looking for romance of a sort. Maybe we mistook the idea of each other for the reality, which was inevitable since we were together for only a week, but it was a week that changed things – my life for the better, and his, as it turned out, for the worse. People say I shouldn't reproach myself, that it's arrogance to do so, but it's hard not to; after all, it was I who encouraged him to dream of

escape, when I could leave while he was forced to stay behind. So when I returned to Romania twelve years later, just over a year after the 1989 revolution, it was with a certain amount of dread as to what I would – or would not – find.

Helena Drysdale, Looking for George (Picador, 1996)

It would be a hard-hearted person who didn't want to read on after that.

A quest does not have to be a serious matter. It can be a bet or a light-hearted whim. If the motive for the journey is to move a fridge around Ireland, or find the perfect boyfriend, it can be just as compelling as a matter of life and death.

BUILDING INTEREST

With all the books that are available to read, a good beginning is an essential way to make sure a reader chooses yours. The good beginning is also likely to be part of what you will use to pitch a book to a publisher. Why this country? Why you? In this competitive age, the writing and the motive for the journey have to stand out immediately. Your first paragraph may be all a busy editor will read. In the interests of catching the eye of this editor research is also important. What has been written about this country before? Why would anyone else be interested in this country? How can your take on the place sustain it through several hundred pages? If the book has a strong beginning many of these questions will be answered. The editor will feel confident that you have a special story and a lively style.

If your research shows that a country has been written about often and that there are grooves in the roadways from the number of fridges that have been pushed around them, then you may need to reconsider your book plan. What is the way that you can write about this place that will make your book exceptional, from the very first paragraph on? Part of the research may involve taking some risks with your time and money. You may not know the motive for your journey until it has been completed. It may not be certain that your idea for a book will work until you have begun some of the travelling. For the book *Show Me the Magic* I began with a curiosity about Benin, but it wasn't until I had spent some time there that I knew the real key to the place was the prevalent belief in voodoo, witchcraft and animist magic. I knew then that my quest was to find out about these things and to see whether I came to believe in any of them. The motive for the journey was discovered en route – the motive that would be strong enough to drive a book that is, rather than the motive we all have, that of feverish curiosity.

Curiosity and the question 'what is Benin really like?' is not enough to sell a book. But a sample chapter and a plan to investigate voodoo did prove to be enough. I could show the editor that I had a definite plan for my book, and had illustrated sufficiently what the style, characters and background to the story would be. Often, people do not know what is going to happen on their travels.

If you sell a proposal about a trip through Madagascar to look for a lost dinosaur and spend the money on a trip to the North Pole, the publisher won't be pleased – unless there is a spectacular 'companion-eaten-by-bears' element to the North Pole story that compensates for your cheekiness. If, however, you go to Madagascar and never meet even a hint of a dinosaur, it is possible to make a good book out of a lively and observant failure. But the further you stray from the original plan, the more irritated your publisher will be, so it is important to be sure you really feel your plan will work when you set out.

Novelists talk of characters' 'taking over' and plot twists occurring to them halfway through the writing. In a travel book characters can take over and events twist into a plot you could not possibly have imagined. Sometimes it can be hard to write a book that matches the original outline you sold to the publisher. Real life can ruin a writer's plans. If it really cannot be helped, and you have to create that lively and observant failure, then it is important to keep rereading the original plan to try to keep a through line in mind, even if you are only explaining why you end up so far from where you started. A through line is your plot in a travel book. If you begin with dinosaurs as your central quest, you do need to refer to them every so often, right up to the end. Even if it is only to remind the reader that events have taken over and you can't concentrate on the original quest. Travel books are often episodic and full of diversions but they still need to have a shape.

FINDING YOUR SELLING POINT

Finding a shape to the story before writing it is vital; finding it before the journey really depends on whether you can afford to gad about for a while without the sobering book contract in your luggage. Publishers seldom go for the proposal that consists of little more than 'I'll just go to such and such a place and see what I find.' Even very well known writers need to be able to say to a publisher, 'I thought I might go here and do such and such.' And they will probably need to provide a convincing paragraph or two on paper as well.

I had a sinking feeling once when tutoring a teacher who thought that she might give up her job for a year, go backpacking round Thailand and write a book about it. Even if she had already written a couple of successful books, this wouldn't have been enough. Possibly if she had been an expert on Thai temples and wanted to see them all, or wanted to discover the truth about Bangkok lady boys, there might have been enough. The more clear the intention of a book is, and how much it specifically relates to the writer, the more likely the book proposal is to sell before the writer starts travelling. If a writer is not established and is only vaguely fascinated by a place, they may have to travel and find their story before even thinking about approaching a publisher.

While travelling or living a life abroad it may be possible to create a situation whereby a publisher approaches you. A book editor heard that I had been living with the Jordanian Bedouin and asked me to write a pitch for a book about my experience. This offer was probably made with some confidence because she knew I'd been writing drama and comedy for some time. I'd also written some articles and made a short radio documentary on the Bedouin. All the same, I had to make a convincing case that I could write a whole book. In the pitch for my book I told my personal story, that the reason for my Jordanian journeys and involvement with the Bedouin was a romance with a Bedouin man. Then, when it came to the writing, I panicked, I didn't want to reveal my inner feelings. Hoping that protecting others would give me an excuse to pull out, I consulted friends in Jordan, thinking that they would object to the book. But they assured me that they didn't mind being in a book, if I changed their names and disguised them just a little. *They* didn't mind; but *I* did.

I rang the editor in a panic. Would it be all right if I just wrote a book about travelling around Jordan? I'd been everywhere in the country so why not?

'Because we already publish a guidebook,' she said, 'Your story is the story. It's a unique insight. Besides, how will you explain how you know the Bedouin so well if the reader doesn't know you nearly married one?' She was right, of course. It couldn't be just a book about Jordan; it had to be my book about Jordan.

Where your journey takes you very often depends on who you are. It may be that you had a slave trading ancestor in Africa and you need to trace him to see how much damage he did. You may have a great aunt who set up a nudist colony in Fiji or was the first woman whaler in Newfoundland. These are the sorts of personal story that give a drive to a travel book. Recently, I met someone who bought natural dyes around the world. She had no interest in travel writing, but what a beautiful book that might have made. A specialist knowledge may mean that the choice of destination is predetermined, but the specialization can give the book its motivation and charm.

One of the reasons people read travel books is to gain an unusual insight on the world. Unusual insights often belong to specialists and enthusiasts. Josie Dew cycles all over the world. Her books are read avidly by fans of cycling and travel alike. If her passion for cycling were not genuine she wouldn't have sustained a fan base of bicycle enthusiasts able to see through someone who had taken a cycling trip purely for the purposes of writing a book. Josie's journeys have an exuberance that would be hard to fake:

> The ride down the wild and rugged sea-lashed coast was truly splendid. The vehement, tempestuous and raging conditions only added to the dramatic flavour of the whole experience as I sped through the spray and streamed along, with the surge of exuberance that comes from being battered and buffeted by the ravages of nature as I rode the terrestrial waves steadily southwards.
>
> Josie Dew, *The Sun in My Eyes* (Time Warner, 2001)

The success of strange adventures undertaken for the purpose of writing a book, such as pushing a fridge around Ireland, depends a great deal on the personality of the author. He or she needs to be somewhat extrovert, to say the least, and definitely have comic ability. The destination could be influenced by the nature of the quest too. In some countries the fridge would just have been stolen on day one. In certain countries the author would have been immediately arrested. In others, the serious-minded population would not have involved themselves with such nonsense. The author made a fair guess that Ireland was the sort of place where there would be enough people willing to join in the joke.

Still Finding It Hard to Start?

The first idea for a book, even the choice of destination, depends on who you are and why you want to go there. These are the questions publishers will ask and the questions you have to ask yourself. If you are stuck about how to get started on a travel book that is more than an account of your backpacking trip around India, a good exercise is, yet again, to make some lists. List the countries you feel drawn to and why. Is there something, or someone, in the country you want to find? Have you a connection to the country? Have you a specialist skill you could use in the country? Is there a record-breaking athletic challenge you could undertake in the country? Perhaps, if you are able to tread a fine writing tightrope, you really dislike the idea of a place and want to change your mind by actually going there.

The next list should develop more from who you are. Are you a sharp, robust P.J. O'Rourke or Bryson type who can get away with doing and saying outrageous or iconoclastic things? Are you unlike the travellers who have written about a country before? Have you spent time in a place forging unusual connections? Are you a champion mountaineer, cyclist, walker, skateboarder on your way to a new challenge? Are you hilariously funny and pretty much able to go anywhere and find fun enough for a whole book? Are you the only person who knows a particular story, or cares about a particular lost treasure, person or city? If the last, you would be lucky these days, but there may be a small, hard-to-access city that is not visited often, and it just so happens your long-lost half brother lives there.

Cross-examine yourself for a while about why you? Why this place? When you are pleased with the answers and confident, then there could be a book in it.

Sometimes, when you stand in a crowded airport at holiday times you might feel very weary at the thought of trying to find an unusual story for a travel book. Haven't all the paths been trodden several times, in day-glo flip-flops? Not necessarily. I do not believe that the world is small. We all live in very different ways. There may be a strange cult in your own country that you want to investigate. Your race or sexuality may make your take on a place unusual and insightful. The more you keep looking, keep thinking, the more likely you are to have one of those wonderful moments where you realize perceptions of our planet and ways of surviving are infinitely varied.

The World Is Not Small

Father was in a talkative mood ... He scooped up little Radya and asked if I'd like to buy her; I said I would but I didn't think I could afford something so precious. Rathwan nodded at me: a good answer. Then his father asked me if we had black babies like this one in England.

'Yes, some.'

'Which are better, black babies or white babies?'

It was like him to ask this kind of question, testing me out. I'd have to find an answer that didn't sound as if I was putting down anything Jordanian but which didn't sound like intelligence-insulting crawling. For instance, when the Syrian had been complaining of a toothache, I'd been asked if I knew of a cure. I'd suggested cloves, an old emergency standby of my mother's, and Rathwan's father had looked contemptuous.

'Cloves? Do you think we don't have dentists?'

So I'd learnt to tread very carefully. This time I said, 'I think black babies are better – they don't show the dirt.'

He roared with laughter, and ordered Yousef to bring us some tea. He asked me what other countries I'd been to and pulled a face when I mentioned Egypt.

'Do you like Jordan or Egypt better?'

There he went again. Questions with potholes.

'Cairo is too crowded and the Bedouin I saw in Egypt were very poor.'

'Yes. And the women are terrible. A friend of mine married an Egyptian woman and she nagged him all the time. Once he refused to tell her where he was going and she took off her shoes and beat him with them. Beat him with her shoes! What do you think of that?'

'Did they have high heels?'

Another roar of laughter. The old man was quiet for a while, then asked a question in a very serious tone.

'He asks if it's true you go back to England soon.'

Yes, sadly it was true.

With richly worded Bedouin largesse, Rathwan's father invited me to return whenever I wanted. I was welcome any time. He hoped I would write to the family and not forget them. I must come back.

I said I very much wanted to return to Jordan.

'*Inshallah*,' he said with deep sincerity. '*Inshallah*.'

On the day I had to fly home, Rathwan was putting my bags into the Toyota. I took a long last look at the desert. Rathwan's father saw what I was doing.

'He asks if in the city where you live you have a house like my aunt's.'

'A bit like it, but smaller.'

A flat actually, no expanse of roof for sunning myself, another block of flats for a view.

Rathwan's father gazed out over the desert and sighed deeply.

'To live in a house,' he said, 'is to live in a grave.'

Annie Caulfield, *Kingdom Of The Film Stars* (Lonely Planet, 1997)

FILLING THE JOURNEY

You know who you are, where you are going and why? But what happens if you land in a strange place and know no one? It may be that you are the type to hang around in bar and get talking to fascinating people. This is not always possible; many women travellers find it a particularly uncomfortable way to find contacts. The intrepid Polly Evans once told me:

> It's really annoying, you know the male traveller writers are all downstairs in the hotel bar meeting smugglers and artists but you're stuck in your room with a book. If you hang around in the bar you have to fiercely read the book so people don't hassle you, so what's the point?

Gender aside, not everyone likes bars, the chances are you will just meet drunken fantasists or unnecessary trouble. The image of the travel writer as a Graham Greene character, discovering political intrigue with glass in hand, may fit a few types still trotting the globe, but the majority are getting up in the morning, clear-headed and anxious to meet people who are not smoke-wreathed and swaying.

CONTACTS

It is really important to scour about for contacts before leaving home. Even if the contact is someone's suburban second cousin living in your destination country. The suburban second cousins may have no real relevance to your enquiries but may still provide a lead, or have a smattering of insider knowledge. They may be lovely people who'll provide you with a friendly bolt-hole when your intrepid adventures and meetings with scary smugglers have worn you to a shred.

The country you are visiting may have press representatives in Britain who could provide useful introductions. The BBC World Service often has experts on a place they can put you in touch with before you leave. But there is a danger with this kind of lead that you will end by meeting journalists, wary of sharing their valuable local sources. On the whole, I've found journalists to be very generous, but they can lead you along paths they have already worn well themselves. They will know what the main stories in a country are and will have followed them up. Travel writers are more likely to need stories outside the news agenda. Usually it is best to have done your own research first into unusual stories you might like to follow and then ask for help finding contacts in the field. Charities and businesses with bases in the country you plan to visit may be able to give you good contacts on the ground. Whom you contact entirely depends on the type of book you are writing, but be prepared to broaden your search. Inevitably you will find more material than you need for your book, but there are always articles to be written as an aside.

Going off at a tangent to your main purpose may lead to new relevant contacts, place your story in a new context, shed an unusual light on your enquiries or simply provide textural background. You may know why you are making your journey but there is no need to be too rigid. Investigating something just off the track builds your knowledge of a country and could provide an unexpected gem of conversation, fact or visual detail. You may feel that simply observing and keeping yourself to yourself is the way to travel. But I wonder how, in a strange place, you can be sure you understand what you are seeing? A mixture of observation and interaction seems to make a richer, more rounded travel book.

INVENTIVE WAYS TO FIND CONTACTS

In general, you have to go out to meet a country, it won't come to you. The easiest people to talk to, or rather listen to, are taxi drivers. This isn't always an expensive way to travel and there is a universal character trait in taxi drivers – they love a captive audience. When they have not got a passenger to talk at, they're waiting somewhere, watching the world go by – and they know the geography of a place better than the average citizen. Sometimes their observations are odd, sometimes dull and predictable, but most of the time a taxi driver is the travel writer's friend.

Reading *The View From The Ground*, a collection of the great Martha Gelhorn's journalism and travel writing, I noticed that she often found out the real state of play in a country by talking to a taxi driver. When she wanted to catch up on the situation in Spain after the Civil War, Gelhorn quickly sought out taxi divers, making sure the driver was of an age to have lived through the war. She had learnt from experience that in their mobile sanctuary taxi drivers feel themselves safe to talk. In one conversation she finds out how the economy is affecting ordinary people and how repressive Franco's regime can be for the average working man. The driver tells her Spanish newspapers are 'novels' and that the only facts reported in them are about football. Gelhorn was also aware that taxi drivers use language far more excitingly than any politicians and can talk their way quickly to the heart of a matter.

If taxis are too expensive, public transport is also the travel writer's friend and the more crowded the better. You will be crushed against all kinds of people with time on their hands to chat. Sometimes, it may be necessary to hire a car. In my view, all the time spent in the car is dead time. Unless your book is actually about driving a small car up Everest and aimed at those interested in driving challenges, when you are in a car you are shielded from the country you are visiting and talking to no one but yourself.

However, if you haven't been able to find contacts before setting out, useful doorsteps to turn up on are those of local action groups, this can again include charities but there may be women's groups and campaigning groups outside the main political parties. Although your line of enquiry may be far removed from religion, a local priest or religious leader can be helpful. Also, whatever your religious background, to attend religious services can be a useful way to see how a community interacts. Attending a small church service in an out of the way place may be a way to make new friends. People might notice that you are a stranger and start talking to you. There is no need to lie and pretend to be religious if you are not, simply admit that you're new in town and this felt like a safe place to be among people. Church and town hall notice boards are good places to look out for small-scale, local events – jumble sales, amateur music evenings, cinema clubs or five-aside football matches. Small events with a small crowd, where a stranger will be noticed, can involve you in a community at a very ordinary, day-to-day level.

Museums are good if you are knowledgeable about art or archaeology and the purpose of your journey is along these lines, but, like libraries, they can be very isolating places. If possible, take a guide or, if this might threaten the budget, at least ask questions of any attendants standing around. You may be the world expert on the exhibit in front of you, but the attendant might provide some local take on it, a peculiar opinion of their own or a nugget of information that suggests you are not the expert you thought you were.

Professional guides are often a little like travel writers themselves. Their purpose is to entertain and hold audience attention. Some countries have strict examination systems to ensure that guides know their facts, but, out in the field, guides quickly learn that style is more important than content. They add a little drama, a little crowd-pleasing myth or gossip. Guides are often colourful characters, amusing to talk to but their patter may not be entirely composed of fact. Sometimes it is worth taking them to one side and asking them whether something they've told you is true or just a good yarn? They might be insulted and insist on their story but occasionally they will confess, tell you the truth and explain why the popular myth has grown up. But if you really need to get something right, you will need to check with the dull experts who've written text books on the subject, rather than basking out in the sunshine listening to the banter of an entertaining guide.

If you are staying in a place where there is an unusual local event, even if it isn't what you have come to see and happens at another season of the year, it can be worth tracking down the organizers and interviewing them. It may lead right to the spiritual heart of a community, or up a cul-de-sac of eccentrics, but you won't know until you ask. In Northern Australia, very bored in a Barrier Reef resort, I noticed that they held an annual rodeo very close to where I was staying. It wasn't rodeo season, but anything was better than watching teenagers in brightly coloured shorts diving drunkenly in and out of my hostel's swimming pool. I rang the rodeo association's chairman, hoping to interview him. He was irritated when he discovered that I was not even vaguely knowledgeable about rodeo but just looking for information on the area. Then he decided that he had better take charge of someone so clueless. He told me all about rodeos in Australia, their history and present-day excitements. He drove me round to meet horse breeders and retired rodeo riders in the area. There were some great characters among his friends. I learnt a lot about the whole community as well as the rodeo riding fraternity. I realized that my new friend epitomized a gruff, macho kindness typical of this part of Australia. Not all spur-of-the-moment telephone calls prove so fruitful, but you never know.

FINDING THE UNUSUAL

If you can't find a way into your main subject or are waiting around for something, it is always worth making a list of topics that may lead you into useful pools of background information. List the things you might need to know about a country, for instance, its religion, politics, diseases, history, art, costume, industry, sports, the status of women, education, crafts, civilities, snobberies, food, entertainment and infrastructure. Pick a topic that interests you, even if it interests you only a little, and see where it leads; at worst it will lead you out of your room and into meeting people.

Peter Moore is a master at making his own entertainment in a country. Even if all he is in search of is himself:

> She was back within minutes with a trim, muscly woman in her thirties who had more than a touch of the Lucy Lius about her. She was not happy at all about being dragged away from the nerve centre of her pirate publishing enterprise.
>
> 'No Peter Moore!', she spat, giving me the sort of withering look Lucy has become famous for, 'Michael Moore. It same!'
>
> I could have suggested that a quick comparison of Michael's and my royalty cheques would quickly clear up that little misunderstanding, but the iciness of her stare and the muscle that twitched in her neck suggested that it wouldn't have been a good idea. Already a proud owner of the entire Michael Moore oeuvre, I took the diplomatic option of buying a copy of the *Lonely Planet Vietnamese Phrasebook*. It cost the full four dollars even though it was a fraction of the size of all the other books, but I'm not ashamed to admit that, frankly, the woman scared me.
>
> The incident, as terrifying as it was, did give me an idea, though. I decided to spend the rest of the day asking every girl selling books in HCMC if they had any books by Peter Moore. At first I let them approach me, in the streets around Pham Nou Lao, pretending that something in their pile of wares had caught

my eye. But by the afternoon I was seeking them out – at the War Remnants Museum, in the internet cafes along De Tham and the restaurants and bars along Dong Khoi, the more affluent part of town. My hope was that when they returned to the warehouse their gang masters would notice a staggering number of requests for books by some bloke called Peter Moore, amongst the usual ones for the latest John Grisham and Joanna Trollope. An illusion that there was a demand for my books would be created and, by the time I got back from the Delta, one of them would be photocopied and have slipped into the Ho Chi Minh City Top 60 as a hot new title. Well, a man can dream.

Peter Moore, Same Same but Different (Amazon Shorts, 2006)

Creating your own entertainment is one way to explore a society. What to explore can depend on your style or your mood on a particular day. It is always important to keep following small glimpses of opportunity in search of a story. Having once worked on an extensive theatre project on mental illness, I am very interested in how different cultures react to the mentally ill. Tracking down the local psychiatric hospital or equivalent of a psychiatric hospital is one of my first expeditions when I am looking for ways to understand a country. The world over, people go mad for the same reasons but they don't go mad in the same way, and they are not treated in the same way. How people go mad and how they are treated can provide an interesting insight into a culture.

In contrast, I like a nice chat about fashion and find that interviewing hairdressers, dressmakers and fabric makers can lead from the gossipy and domestic to wider issues such as the rights of women, or the state of the world cotton industry.

A country's education system is a way to examine the lives of children, families and gain insight into political systems. Looking for some action in Cuba, Martha Gelhorn once barged into the first secondary school that she saw. She announced that she was a foreign journalist and would like to sit in on a class to observe the teaching methods. This provoked considerable confusion, as it would in any school anywhere, and she was taken to see the officials at the Education Department. After a few run-ins with obstructive bureaucrats, she was invited to make a formal visit to a school. Gelhorn was a little embarrassed to be greeted by singing children with bouquets, but she got her chance to sit in on class. She had conversations with teachers, pupils and even the caretaker. Her initial impetuous arrival at a school enabled her to see the country's bureaucracy at work and to see it overridden by the natural friendliness of the people. By opening that school door she found a great deal more to write about than how a secondary school class was conducted.

Creating situations and asking questions may lead you into a tangle of bureaucracy, or lead you to an enchanting and informative welcome. Even if none of us will ever be a Martha Gellhorn, the trick is not to waste time, but be bold and be prepared to create and follow a tangent. I know many writers like sitting alone in their rooms but, when travelling to make a book, you do need to get yourself out and about.

Be Bold

It is not always easy but I have found, with a few deep breaths, it is worth the wear and tear on the nerves to be bold, even downright cheeky. I have a BBC staff pass that I often use to get an interview, although I have to cover the information at the bottom of the card that would reveal the fact that it allows me to visit the BBC drama department and is about two years out of date. You could invent a magazine or newspaper if you feel you need an employer's credentials. My out-of-date card has gained me access to local pop stars, an Arabian princess and, once, to a president. Sometimes the honest truth of telling people you are writing a travel book can open more doors than any suspicion that you are a journalist. A travel writer can be seen as connected to the world of tourism, a positive thing for a country – whereas journalists are often perceived as dubious characters in search of bad news and scandal. There are occasions when you have to say nothing or people will clam up; you have to pretend to be an idling tourist and hide your notebook.

I have seldom been to a place where writing a book caused real alarm. In Benin, my chatty taxi driver friend Isidore completely changed his attitude to me when he knew I was writing a book. I was no longer a rich, idling tourist, I was a useful working person who deserved help and respect. In Northern Ireland, where I expected suspicion, I was greeted with open enthusiasm when I explained that I was looking to write a book about something other than The Troubles.

In countries that have been isolated, been through very difficult and dangerous times, people are often surprisingly willing to talk. They want to tell you about the aspects of the country that never make the headlines; they want someone to record the positive and accomplished side of their lives. Or they want someone to record their pain. If you don't ask, you'll never know. The worst person to talk to is anyone in government offices, from the lowest grade of civil servant to the president of the country. The lowly are nervous, or jobs-worths; the exalted seldom got to where they are by telling anyone the truth. Sometimes it is necessary to talk to bureaucrats and rulers to get access or to get the official line. A politician's version of events can sit in nice contrast to a taxi driver's or a hairdresser's – but the latter two are likely to be far more truthful and interesting.

When I did interview a president, he gave me the usual evasive political blether about his bad governance, but revealed himself when I asked him about football and where his rather startling furniture came from. He was self-effacing about himself as an amateur footballer and surprisingly enthusiastic about his furniture – he'd chosen it himself and could tell me where to order similar tables and chairs. I suddenly saw how he had, give or take a few assassinations of rivals, charmed his way into power. If someone isn't telling you anything interesting, shift them on to an unlikely tangent and you might find something more revealing than the party line.

When I was in Jordan I was fascinated by a locally produced soap opera about the trials and tribulations of a Bedouin family. Local television or radio programmes, news and newspapers can be entertaining and informative ways to research a country if you absolutely cannot find anyone to talk to. If you have a specialist interest that may not be the main theme of your book, it can lead you into meeting people, be it the local butterfly-collecting society, an exercise class or an astronomers' club.

Drawing people towards you is often a useful way to get involved. Alastair Scott travelled the Caribbean wearing a kilt because it was an ice-breaker and he felt it was fair: if he told people something about Scotland, then it was polite to ask them questions about their home. In many places I have found having blue eyes and white blonde hair is enough to draw a curious crowd – although sometimes in Africa the sight of me terrified small children.

There is always the unusual travelling companion, that fridge again. Or, not that I'm comparing them to a piece of kitchen furniture, children as companions can be a logistical difficulty but will draw people to you, make you instantly protected in a community and involve you in aspects of life the more traditional traveller might never see. Don't feel that you have to leave them behind or that travel writing is not for the parent. Dervla Murphy travelled with her daughter Rachel from around Rachel's sixth birthday. To travel with a child makes a journey more unusual. It takes the journey away from the old notion that travel writing is a job for the athletically heroic, braving the unknown. A child, even on the walk to the post office, can have their own unusual observations to make. They're no more likely to get hot, tired and irritable than some adult companions and they are more entertaining company than a fridge.

If you cannot find anyone to talk to or cannot summon up the nerve to barge in somewhere and force a conversation, go out to a public place and eavesdrop. Go to a café, launderette or take a bus journey. Look, listen, keep busy and thereby collect far more than you'll need for the book. There will be plenty of time for sitting alone in your room when you are writing.

FILLING THE PAGES

LOOKING

Although the last chapter stressed the importance of interacting with people and listening, the other essential thing to do is to look. Simply walk about, looking. Look at the larger view and at the detail. This is how the descriptive and reflective parts of your story will occur to you. A strong piece of description needs variety and precision. There is a way of looking in order to write well that is more intense than our normal gawking around. What colour is something really? What is its texture? What does it remind you of? How does looking at it make you feel? Do the words you are going to use sound like the mood of a place?

In her book *A Sultan in Oman*, Jan Morris describes an alley in an Arab town as 'velvety'. Her walk through the alley is restful, surrounded by old stone walls and fruit trees. The 'velvety' atmosphere is created by the accumulating detail in the description. The heart of a powerful description is to draw on something unexpected but accurate, such as using 'velvety' to describe an alley.

To avoid cliché, a search for the unexpected is essential. When you look at a place, does it remind you of somewhere else? Perhaps you're in an intimate bar that feels more like a private chapel in an Elizabethan stately home. Perhaps you're in a bar so steely and modern you feel as though you're in an industrial kitchen.

What a place reminds you of may also indicate the feeling it creates. Is it a restful or jarring atmosphere? Does it remind you of somewhere comforting or disturbing? Looking, thinking and reflecting emotionally on a place are all part of the slow process of finding the right description.

Of course, sometimes the right description comes to you in a flash. The memory that a sight triggers occurs to you immediately. This is lucky, but more often a seemingly effortless description will have to be worked at, as if you are turning a musical instrument to exactly the right tone. A description might not necessarily be of a place. There may be animals, people, trains, planes and automobiles along your way that need describing.

If a thing is moving, how is it moving? Can a word from the mechanical or electronic world be used to describe an animal? Can a description from nature describe concisely how a machine operates? Can human characteristics be applied to an aeroplane? Swapping categories around can summon up an exciting description, or simply be ridiculous. As an exercise, trawling the non-animate world for a description of an animal can be interesting. Sometimes the inappropriateness is jarring. Sometimes, swapping categories brings a thing to life. As an obvious suggestion, the vocabulary useful for a description of a shark might be found in the world of metallic things. There is also a need to find description for smells and sounds as well as sights. It is important to be accurate and yet original; to be interesting without being too contrived. Again, swapping categories can be useful – is the animal making a noise associated with a human emotion? Is the sound you hear in nature reminiscent of something machine-made? Does the sound remind you of a taste? Does a smell have a texture, or remind you of the look of something? Does a smell provoke a complicated reminiscence or a feeling? An interesting exercise can be to find something in the categories of each of the senses: sight, sound, smell, taste and touch, and describe it in terms appropriately belonging to another sense.

BEING DESCRIPTIVE

When I start to write a descriptive passage, I know that I am not writing in my strongest area and I start to panic – there are not enough adverbs or adjectives and that's that. It is important, however to remember that metaphor can save you from a tired piece of description. Although it can be possible to be too obscure with a reference in a metaphor – 'His hair was the colour of a day-old marmoset.' This is not a reference point most people have, although I think it is fine to say, 'His hair looked as though he'd thrown a marmoset on his head as he left the house.' In this case it does not matter how much we know about the look of marmosets. Most of us know that they are small, furry animals and we get the idea that the man has peculiar hair.

Description can be too precise. I once introduced a character in a book as, 'looking like Wesley Snipes'. My editor did not know who Wesley Snipes was and so had no idea what I was trying to describe. She made me find a more detailed description from general reference points, so that later, when I mentioned that the character looked like him, those unfamiliar with the film star already had a picture of the character. In general, saying that someone looks like someone else is a little lazy, unless the resemblance is peculiar or significant, a Russian old lady who looks like Stalin, for example. This mention of a name seems fine as it refers to someone with a well-known face. An old French lady with a look of Jean-Luc Godard might not work well, bizarre though it might be, because it does not refer to a man almost universally recognizable. A good metaphor should have the effect of making a reader say 'of course'. It is something they haven't thought of but can see that it is exactly right.

In his book *Sunrise with Seamonsters*, Paul Theroux describes the way giraffes gallop 'as if they're about to come apart at any second'. This is very simple and captures more about the giraffe than the way it gallops. Like much good description, this also has a tone of voice. In this case, when thinking of the giraffe it is clear that Theroux feels fondness and amusement.

The tone of a description could be fearful, resentful, awed, envious, passionate – and so on. This is a subtle thing, depending on context but also on the type of words used. 'Her wedding dress was like an explosion at a candy floss stall,' tells us about the dress in a very different tone of voice from 'her wedding dress was a shade of pink found in happy memories of childhood at the seaside'.

As an exercise, it is worth describing something according to the different emotions it provokes. Are you looking at a view that is pleasant, disturbing, melancholic or enraging? Without mentioning your emotion, the sort of words you use in the description add a layer, they bring a description alive with a feeling. For instance: 'The small bedroom had a carpet that he just knew would show itself to be stained if he turned the main light on. A coat of uneven cream paint had been applied over 1970s wallpaper. The bedspread was a red candlewick he associated with a long-dead great aunt who'd lost her mind and wandered, urine-smelling, through the suburbs of Leicester.'

This room evokes the worst kind of feeling. Whereas the next room would cheer the visitor up: 'Just across the fields, he could see the thin blue line of the sea. A smell of new-mown hay came up from the fields, along with the sounds of birds calling to each other. He didn't know the type of birds they were – that was the sort of thing he'd known as a boy but had lost somewhere during his hectic life of city thoughts. There was clean white paint on the window frame, a delicate flower in the wallpaper, and more clean white for the sheets on the big square bed. He set his suitcase down on the honey-coloured wood of the floorboards. He should begin to unpack but wanted to stand a moment longer, looking out through that white framed window.'

Finding the right description can take time. Yet a forced description is worse than no description.

If you are struggling to describe something, perhaps it doesn't need to be described. Sometimes, mentioning that something is 'red' or 'big' or 'ugly' is enough. Better one strong word than five floundering ones.

DESCRIPTION IN ACTION

It is important to choose carefully where to place description. If the description is meandering and detailed, it should occur at an appropriately contemplative moment in the story – at a moment where the story needs to take a moment to breathe. Too much detailed description can delay an action scene. In an action scene there can be description too but the words are likely to be sharp, in sentences that keep moving quickly. For instance: 'His horse charged into the arena, then he pulled it up short. The horse fought him but he held it still. He looked at the crowd with a challenge in his eyes, then he flung his heels in the air, leapt to the ground and picked up the bag of gold. He raised it in a fist, shouted abuse at the crowd, waiting for the rain of picnic debris and insults that he knew would fall on him. He began to laugh, realizing they were too shocked to react. He turned his back and walked out, leaving his sweat flecked horse behind. He didn't even care about the horse now.'

Sometimes, to torment writing students I give them a photograph and ask them to describe the landscape. I ask them to imagine why they are in the landscape. Are they being chased? Are they trudging along with a broken heart? Are they lost? Are they gleefully strolling along on holiday? Does the landscape heighten or alter their mood? In the description they have to include all five senses and give me one surprising piece of information, such as the cardigan in this passage: 'There were so many bluebells among the trees it was almost obscene. Too bright, too accusingly reminding him to count his blessings. Although there was clean, warm sunlight, the woods had their usual musty smell. He came to the spot where Olivia had thrown off a cardigan she didn't like. It must still be in the green undergrowth somewhere, mouldy. Then he saw it, a red sleeve hooked on brambles. He went to touch it. The distressing feel of damp wool. He thought about rescuing it, a souvenir. He left it and walked on to the station. The gum in his mouth had lost its flavour. Rebelliously he spat it out in a high arc as he walked.'

Tormenting yourself at home with this exercise is a good way to get the descriptive powers straining to do their best. Particularly for those, like me, who tend to hear conversations in a place and notice little else. Not that hearing a conversation is not important, dialogue brings a page alive. How people are in a conversation can give a vivid picture of them as much as a description. Changing a piece of reported information into dialogue can transform it. Instead of writing, 'The guide told me that the tower was five thousand years old ...' make the guide become a person, give him his own words. Did he have a particular speech pattern, a barely audible voice, a strange gesture he used repeatedly? Information put into dialogue immediately becomes more dramatic. Instead of telling us, 'We had an argument with the annoying ticket inspector and nearly missed the train' to write down the argument could build dramatic tension, be full of atmosphere and give a picture of your characters as well as the annoying ticket inspector. We would also be able to conclude for ourselves that he was annoying without being told.

Writing dialogue brings in other people and means that we are not trapped alone with the writer, their thoughts and observations all the time. The book will change tone more often and have more pace. To construct a piece of dialogue well on the page it is useful to remember the trick of imagining that you are a film director. Who is speaking now? To whom ? What are they doing while they are speaking? Is the rhythm of their speech tense and staccato, careful or relaxed? What is the mood of the scene – aggressive? melancholic? romantic?

The question of using 'he said', 'she said' can be a matter of taste. Once a scene is up and running and the characters are established it should be clear most of the time who is speaking. More often than not, we do not need to be told someone is speaking 'reluctantly' or 'angrily'. The speech should tell us that.

Occasionally an adverb is necessary. Occasionally 'said' can be replaced with words and phrases such as 'muttered', 'shouted', 'screamed', 'growled', but it should be the words spoken that matter more than these markers. Similarly, I find replacing 'said' with words such as 'opined' or 'mused' can sound archaic and contrived. I can almost hear the writer remembering an old-fashioned primary school exercise to replace 'said' in as many different ways as possible. Out of primary school, the point is really to ensure that we barely notice the punctuating 'saids' or their variants and to let the dialogue flow.

The more sub-texts and story that can be built into a dialogue scene, the more vivid it will be. Imagine the scene in the extract below if I had simply reported: 'Dinner was interrupted by an eccentric old lady who claimed the waitresses had robbed her earlier in the day. She made a fuss for about an hour, pestering all the customers to take her side. In the end I felt sorry for her and gave her some money. She went away but she was still complaining about how the waitresses had misused her.'

In this case it would have been very difficult to express the emotion and include the political asides without going through the whole scene of recorded action and dialogue. I have tried to build a picture of all the characters in the scene, even the captain who has so few lines but his contribution is essential. (Just as a note, *Yovo* is the word for a white person in this part of Africa and Dahomey was the name of the state until the 1970s.)

In the evening the trees around the garden restaurant were strung with fairy lights and Natasha, the waitress told us it was chicken or chicken for dinner.

Natasha was a hefty Togolese girl in a T-shirt and the same baggy, three-quarter length cotton khaki trousers as I was wearing, so we'd bonded over this. Natasha's trousers were very important in the events of the evening. As was her very small sweet face. This face, along with her chirpy smile, didn't quite disguise a girl you could tell had initiated a lot of brawls in the school playground, and won. In contrast, Estelle, older and the boss, was a slim, gentle Togolese who looked like her life had been one sadness after another, borne with fortitude but increasing weariness. She seemed to be the sort of woman who made Isidore go all melty round the edges ...

As Estelle went to cook dinner, Natasha attended to a newly arrived Beninois army captain. Just as she put the drinks on the table, a high-pitched shrieking started from the railway tracks behind the restaurant garden. Natasha charged out, bellowing in French, 'Get lost! Go away or I'll sort you out! Go away, I told you, go!' Schoolyard Natasha emerged. She stormed back in and started crossly roaring something kitchenwards. Estelle made a soothing response.

The captain asked Natasha what was going on. She straddled a chair at our table to let us all in on the drama. Early in the evening, an old woman had come in, walked across the restaurant and dropped her purse – coins rolled everywhere. The old woman burst into tears. Feeling sorry for her, Natasha and Estelle had crawled round the floor – *crawled* – for ten minutes, collecting the coins for her until they were sure there were no more to find. The old woman then started a hue and cry, calling Natasha a thief, Estelle a whore, claiming she was 850 francs (75 pence) short and that the girls had taken it. She'd gone on and on until they'd had to shout at her and chase her out – now she was back with the same story. Wailing outside, saying the women had robbed her.

'Last time I help anyone,' Natasha concluded. She swung off her chair and went to yell abuse at the voice from the railway tracks.

Before Natasha could catch her, the voice from the tracks materialized in our midst, sobbing and holding out a handful of coins to the captain.

'My dear general,' she sobbed. 'I can see you have a kind face; please help me. These Togolese whores have stolen my money. This is all I have. I had eight hundred and fifty francs and they took it.' Then, in a very different tone of voice, she shrieked at Estelle who was coming from the kitchen to see the show. 'There's the other whore! A fat whore and a thin whore from Togo!'

To finish his drink in peace, the captain said, 'That's enough now,' handed her 1,000 francs (£1) and told her to go home.

Natasha exploded. 'Don't give her anything, she's a liar!' She snatched the 1,000 francs and gave it back to the soldier.

A siren scream came out of the old woman. 'My money! You thieving prostitutes. You see how they are with an old woman? My family have lived in Porto Novo since the time of Dahomey and my father was a customs officer and my mother was a doctor. I'm not used to this, I'm a proper person from this kingdom and now I'm being set upon by savage foreign whores.'

The captain tried to give her the money again, signalling Natasha to back off.

'You're a liar!' Natasha yelled in the woman's ear. 'Take what this man's giving you and get lost!'

The old woman flinched tight and sobbed harder. Real tears down a wrinkled, refined little face. 'Oh, what happened to my life? Oh, my dear white lady … .' She came over to me. 'Look how these savage whores are treating me. My dear white lady, I am from a good family, my family knew many whites, they came to our house when I was a child. And now look at me, please help me and protect me, white lady, please.'

Her tears and her little scrumpled doll-face nipped at my feelings as much as they had the captain's. There was a polish about her that did support her story of social fall; her clothes were smart, her hair carefully plaited, she had gold earrings and the little leather clip-purse she brandished as Exhibit A was shiny new. Her fall had clearly not taken her to sleeping in the gutter or neglecting to wash. Whatever madness had overtaken her seemed too sad to merit the jeering imitation Natasha had just started – 'Oh, my dear white lady …'

I reached for my purse. Natasha shouted, '*Yovo*, don't!' Isidore frowned at me disapprovingly, the old woman screamed at Natasha, 'Who are you, you whore with your big head, your eyes like a sheep and your mouth like a bat!'

Natasha was too bewildered by the insult to fire back more than a quiet echo. 'Mouth like a bat?'

'You whore with your banana-planter's trousers, you don't even dress respectably, fat girl in the banana-planter's trousers of a whore!'

My banana-planter's trousers obviously didn't make me a whore, because the old lady came tugging at my arm. 'Help me, dear white lady, help me please. They stole my money.'

I gave her 1,000 francs; I couldn't help it. Natasha decided that was the end – she grabbed the old woman by the shoulders and frogmarched her out to the railway tracks. 'You've got her money, it's over, now get lost, you old bitch!'

It wasn't over.

From outside the old lady kept wailing, 'My dear white, she's hurt me.'

Isidore told me off about the money. Natasha started throwing stones in the direction of the railway tracks. Estelle stopped her. 'Leave her, Natasha, she'll go.'

There were more plaintive cries from outside, while Isidore and the captain concluded that the old woman probably did this all over town, counting on the softhearted and her ability for relentless-nuisance value to keep herself fed.

Isidore turned to me, genuinely puzzled. 'Why did you give her money? You saw the captain did the same. It's what she wanted.'

I shrugged. 'She made me sad.'

'Me too,' said the captain.

Natasha flopped into a chair by a vacant table. 'It's me that's sad. Imagine being told you've got a bat's mouth. What's a bat's mouth like anyway?'

'And we've got banana-planter's trousers,' I reminded her.

She kissed her teeth. 'Yeah. Old fool. These are high fashion, aren't they?' The thought of high-fashion garments being so mocked propelled her to a final roar into the night against the receding complaints of the perhaps not so mad old woman, with 2,000 francs' profit clipped in her purse.

Annie Caulfield, *Show Me the Magic* (Viking Penguin, 2002)

As the scene happened I knew it was a gift, a wonderful moment where strangers are drawn together by their situation. The scene was full of interesting characters. It was sad as well as funny. Writing it was something of a challenge all the same. I had to make it clear why I changed sides emotionally a number of times. I had to do justice to all the vivid characters. I had to keep a balance between making it clear what all the characters were doing and saying, while not cluttering the scene up with any of their less relevant remarks or actions. There was the idyllic setting to bring in to the background, as well as trying capture relevant details of the look and sound of all the people involved.

This scene has busy and quiet moments in it, although overall it is a noisy scene, full of comings and goings. A scene of a different tone follows it, just to give the reader a rest.

Varying the type of scene is an important consideration. A noisy time may need a quiet time to follow it, or an escalation of the noise to a climax. A long period of the writer's observing or reflecting may need breaking up with a dialogue or action scene. Two people talking may need livening by moving to scenes of crowds, or a third party becoming involved in the scene.

HUMOUR

Sometimes the people you come across, or situations you become involved in, provide you with a ready-made comic incident. The best of these is where you are part of the scene, perhaps a catalyst and therefore laughing with people rather than at them. There are still writers who jeer at the comical foreigner, sometimes for being foreign in their own country. In my humour I try to remember that the only comical foreigner in the room is me.

A few times I have quoted bizarre translations into English on menus, or have been unable to resist recoding someone's eccentric grasp of English but I am trying to drop this cheap trick now. The real joke is that I am in someone else's country, unable to read or speak their language. A test I've started to use on myself is to ask, would this scene be funny if everyone in it was English? If the answer is yes, then I know I've got some hope of a universal depth to the humour, rather than it relying on comedy foreigners.

Other than that, what makes a piece of writing funny is a real 'how long is a piece of string' question. One key is that if you find something funny, everyone else might not find it as funny as you do. So the best thing is not to labour the joke. Deliver it quickly and then move on.

When I was a stand-up comedy writer, I learnt that the position of one word in a sentence can make a huge difference. The word you need to get at the end of the sentence is the key word to the joke. As a classic example, don't say: 'and then my trousers split.' The funnier version is: 'then I split my trousers.' The latter works better because 'trousers' is a funny word and shouldn't be wasted. If you read it aloud you will hear that 'split' brings the sentence inflection down at the end, whereas 'trousers' brings the inflection up. An up inflection is funnier and climactic. The humorous parts of your writing will really benefit from being read aloud. If the word order is just that shade wrong, it is easier to hear than to see.

A few years ago there was a fashion for travel writing to be incessantly funny, but it isn't essential. If humour really doesn't fit with the story you are trying to tell, it is better not to shoehorn it in. I think it's also fatal to include things that you imagine other people will find funny but didn't really appeal to your sense of humour. Perhaps you might be tempted to write your own version of a Bill Bryson style comical rant – even though you're really too mild-mannered to be amused by cumulative insult. In that case the rant is unlikely to ring true. Humour is too personal to fake.

TONE

The tone of the whole book is the next thing to consider. Is it full of action? Is there tension running through the story? Do you use a lot of dialogue? If there is more dialogue than prose, you could decide to risk writing in the present tense. Or you may feel you need the more usual, more reflective past tense. Belgian writer Lieve Joris uses the present tense very effectively in her work *The Gates of Damascus*. Her Syrian friends in Damascus are living in permanent fear of the secret police, so the present tense is useful to convey the ongoing paranoia. It keeps the sense that something is about to happen. It is tricky to handle but is suitable for a personal story where there are a lot of events and the writer uses a large proportion of dialogue.

Looking back over the whole book, is there a balance between activity and reflection; light and shade; the writer's thoughts and interaction? When you re-read the work, the pages where you feel your attention wandering may be where you need a change of tone. Possibly you can divert out of a narrated story and into a dialogue scene and back again.

Where you have set out to write a poetic and whimsical book, it can be jarring if you suddenly become light-hearted and gossipy. Similarly, in a book that is overall a comic travelogue, it can seem strange to launch suddenly into rich, literary, referenced prose. This does not mean that you have to keep to one tone of voice throughout, but you may need to slide in and out of the changes. If you have been joky up to a certain point, explain why your mood suddenly becomes deeper and more reflective. Perhaps you are told a sobering tale or come across a landscape so stunning that you find yourself contemplating your mortality. Let the reader make the journey through your change of mind and mood with you. Then, when you are more cheerful or flippant again, make it clear what shifts your mood.

When your book has been quite serious and distant in tone, don't suddenly jump out on the reader with a personal anecdote. Move in stages from the general to the personal. For example:

> The recent history of Northern Ireland has been sad and scarred. In between those television news images and dark editorials, people have been living varied and often surprisingly happy lives. They've done other things than live through The Troubles. When I hear gloomy opinions of Belfast, I always think of my pipe-smoking cousin who lives in West Belfast. After years as a teacher, my cousin retrained as a juggler and unicyclist and now works in street festivals around the world. Quite why Mary started smoking a pipe at the same time as the unicycling began, I've never really fathomed. Perhaps it relieves the stress that even such a singular character can feel in the day to day uncertainties of Belfast life.

When we are done with Mary we can make a gentle transition back to the general and more serious. For instance, 'Like many, Mary has carved out her own niche in Northern Ireland but there are those on estates like the Brownlow in Craigavon who would have to be very determined and courageous to escape in any way from a culture of violence and drug dependency ...' Moving out of your general tone for a little lightness, or personal involvement, is no bad thing, as long as the reader can see the logical progression of your thoughts. There is no hurry; but be sure the reader can feel confident that you are leading them into an aside for a good reason and that there will be something worth seeing.

Although I believe that narrators are never neutral and who they are influences their books, some are more neutral than others. How much of yourself you put in the story depends on your style, as we have already discussed. It also depends on the nature of the journey. If you are writing about an expedition there are other people besides yourself to write about. What you are looking for, or looking at, may be more important than how you feel about it. Whether or not to remove yourself as much as possible from the narrative entirely depends on what your story is about.

In his page-turning story of living at the Parisian bookstore Shakespeare & Co., *Books, Baguettes and Bedbugs*, Jeremy Mercer gives a tension to his story by telling us something of his life before his journey begins. We know he has had to leave home in a hurry, there are gangsters trying to kill him. We know he has no money left and has to make his life in the bookshop work. Where it has been established that a writer must keep travelling and has no option to flee for the comforts of home, a journey becomes very powerful. Although the circumstances of his life get a little easier through the book, Mercer's emotional problems haunt his journey. He uses an interesting technique when he wants to describe a time of misery and self-loathing in his life. He finds an extended metaphor for his feelings about himself, far more effective than a bald statement of his mood. He is swimming in the sea and notices a wasp in the water. It is struggling pitifully. Mercer wants to lift it out of the water but is worried about getting stung. A couple of times he flicks the wasp in the air but it falls back into the water. He still daren't just scoop it out of the water to save it, so the wasp drowns. He feels this is all typical of him; he means well, but never tries hard enough.

Showing, Not Telling

Show rather than tell is a useful mantra to have running through your head as you write. Show yourself doing something or tell us what you said rather than explaining your emotions. We shall gather what you felt from the action or speech. Even if you don't do something but only think about it, it is better to keep the tone active. If you were angry it is better to say, 'I wanted to hit him' than draw out the moment and feeling that needs sharpness with 'I was so angry I felt as though I wanted to hit him.' Similarly, 'I could have hugged everyone in the room' is more lively and evocative than 'I was deliriously happy.' There are circumstances where adding an emotional response deadens the story you are trying to tell by overstating the case. If you are travelling through a place where something terrible is happening, a famine or the political repression of women, describing what you see, very precisely and carefully, will evoke enough emotion. Your own responses do not need to be added. If you are at a jubilant carnival, show how it feels rather than explain. Who is dancing, how? What is the music like? The costumes? The smells? The expressions on other people's faces?

Honesty is important but too much can be tedious and unnecessary. Not all the minutiae and irritations of a journey are interesting. Too much of them can distract from the drive of the story. Nevertheless, a writer's thoughts along the way can also provide a pleasant recognition of the inconveniences and discomforts of travel. Again, show what those discomforts are. Write the dialogue for the conversation with the irritating passenger in your train coach; describe what your face looks like after a long-haul flight; describe the terrible breakfast rather than simply telling us that it was terrible. None of us are completely affable and accepting of life's setbacks all the time, so it can be heartening to know that we're not alone.

Explaining yourself as you go along is a good way to keep the reader confident about your writing ability. If there is a change of tone, or even a major change of plan in the journey, explain what has happened: 'Although this was supposed to be a camping trip through China, the goats' eating our tent meant we did have to spend a fortnight in hotels and inns until we found a replacement. Buying a tent in China is not easy ... .'

Inconveniences of Train Travel

The cars are built in compartments that hold eight persons each. Each compartment is partially subdivided, and so there are two tolerably distinct parties of four in it. Four face the other four. The seats and backs are thickly padded and cushioned and are very comfortable; you can smoke, if you wish; there are no bothersome peddlers; you are saved the infliction of a multitude of disagreeable fellow-passengers. So far so well. But then the conductor locks you in when the train starts; there is no water to drink, in the car, there is no heating apparatus for night travel; if a drunken rowdy should get in, you could not remove a matter of twenty seats from him, or enter another car, but above all, if you are worn out and must sleep, you must sit up and do it in naps, with cramped legs and in a torturing misery that leaves you withered and lifeless the next day – for behold they have not that culmination of all charity and human kindness, a sleeping car, in all France.

Mark Twain, *The Innocents Abroad* (Chatto & Windus, 1869)

THE WHOLE BOOK

Remember to keep checking the beginning of the book. Are you ambling too far away from the story you promised the reader? Do you need to blend the change of course into the general shape more smoothly? Setting your book to one side for at the very least a week and then reading it through is a good way to see the wood for the trees – to see how the story overall holds together. Have you taken too long on an interesting but only vaguely relevant tangent? If you have set out on a quest it is important to check that you have a clear enough line. Have you found out what you meant to find out? If not, have you clearly explained why not?

If strong characters have been introduced into the story, do we need to know what happens to them in the end? Have you used the characters in the most effective way? We need to see them in action and to hear them talking more than we need you to say, 'so and so was a bitter, taciturn man'. Much better to have him do or say something that illustrates this. Reveal characters rather than explain them. And do not abandon them without a proper end to their participation in the story. Even if they just appear to say one line and then slam out of the room. If a character comes in, we need to see them leave at some point, or know that they deliver their line as they pass through to another room.

If a room is crowded, this may be all we need to know about the 'extras' in the scene. They are simply a crowd. Perhaps the room is crowded with people dressed as Mae West, in which case we need to know at some point that there is a Mae West impersonators convention starting in the bar later. Whoever is in the scene needs to be examined carefully. Do you need them? Or perhaps they are a crowd of strangers, nothing to do with your scene about being told the news of a tragic death but their inappropriateness, Mae West impersonators for example, may be a useful counterpoint to make your scene more poignant.

In travel books there are many passing encounters; we don't know the past of all of the characters, the details of their lives nor what becomes of them after they wander off. It is important to make their brief appearances in the story vivid and worth the words. Did they tell you something important? Did they upset you? Did they delay you, rescue you or make you laugh? If they are just standing around, cluttering up the scene with one insignificant remark about your near fatal car crash, humiliation in the post office or triumphant arrival at the North Pole on a skateboard, then write them out.

Often there might actually be three people in a scene, but if only two matter then overlook the third. No one wants to hear the waiter say, 'More bread rolls?' in a love scene, unless it is a comical break in the mood. If you are on an expedition and the group is large, it may be worth losing a few of the characters who keep themselves in the background. You could mention so-and-so and so-and-so who were just quiet members of the group – but once they are introduced we will wonder what happened to them. You will feel obliged to mention them every so often. If they are written out, you can concentrate on the characters that move the story on and had significance for you on the trip.

Keep no unnecessary characters and keep the story moving. If you are stuck at a border for three days, give us the essence of the experience rather than a blow-by-blow account that makes us feel that we have been reading about the incident for three days. Let the reader know how the characters feel, but not all the time. Sometimes we just need them to be getting on with the journey.

If your journey has been one of frustrations and dead ends, these can make a frustrating read unless the tone of them varies considerably. Often it is better to pick the best examples of the culs-de-sac you ran into and imply that there were many more. When you reread your finished manuscript and found passages that were interesting but which slow the book down or seem irrelevant, look at it as ruthlessly as you would look at a suitcase that won't close. Something will have to come out and that's that.

It isn't necessary to come home at the end of the book journey. End it where your quest is over, or on the incident that you feel encapsulates your experience. The reader can assume that you got home safely. If you did not, or you ran away with a Mongolian tribesman and are now typing in a yurt, then that is another matter entirely and perhaps we need to know.

To use the luggage reference again in a different way – don't do this in your book – think of your travel book as something to be slipped into someone's hand luggage. They don't want a huge tome weighing them down and making them doze off over their airline snacks. They want a trim volume, without a spare word or a superfluous thought, and a sense of regret when they reach the last page. They could happily have read fifty more pages. They have really enjoyed travelling with you and might travel with you again.

SOME PRACTICALITIES ON THE JOURNEY

To those bred under an elaborate social order few such moments of exhilaration can come as that which stands at the threshold of wild travel. The gates of the enclosed garden are thrown open, the chain at the entrance of the sanctuary is lowered, with a wary glance to right and left you step forth and, behold! The immeasurable world. The world of adventure and of enterprise, dark with hurrying storms, glittering in raw sunlight, an unanswered question and an unanswerable doubt hidden in the fold of every hill ... So you will leave the sheltered close, and, like the man in the fairy story, you feel the bands break that were riveted about your heart as you enter the path that stretches across the rounded shoulder of the earth.

Gertrude Bell, *The Desert and the Sown* (1907)

I hope I have established that, in my view, you don't need to be a Gertrude Bell to be a travel writer. In fact, although I agree with the sentiment, and feel very cheeky indeed to be saying it, I think the extract above shows that the great Gertrude Bell may have been much better at travelling than she was at writing. I do not believe that you need to be a great traveller to write a good travel book. Today, you need to be an observant, curious storyteller in this genre, but there is no need, unless it is the kind of thing that inspires you, to endure SAS-level physical difficulty and biological-warfare-level toilet facilities. One of the most successful travel books in recent years was Bill Bryson's *Notes from a Small Island* – mostly an account of English bed-and-breakfasts.

Just meeting and trying to understand a person from a completely different culture can be difficult enough and more than enough to write about. Having almost always lived in central London, I recently spent some months living in a small town in Kent and I was completely baffled by the neighbours. They were so friendly and helpful it made me completely paranoid. I suspected they were dropping by to case the joint before robbing it. What did they want with me, they didn't know me from Adam, or Eve? They wanted nothing, of course, they were just behaving the way neighbours behave outside London.

It is important to find ways to get involved with a place, finding contacts, setting up appointments, but I set a lot of store by just hanging out in a destination. A radio correspondent once told me that, no matter how much of a hurry he is in, he tries to spend the first evening or morning in a place simply walking around and just looking. First impressions matter. As what you are looking at is strange to you, it will appear vivid in a way it never will again. Have you ever had that experience of walking around a place now familiar and suddenly having the strange flashback sensation of remembering how it looked the very first time you saw it? Significant features of a stranger's face are much easier to recall than the familiar creases and moles on the face of a loved one. On our first look at a face we note one or two striking things immediately; to describe a face we know, we have to rack our brains to think of the features that stand out from the well-known whole.

Bryson's encounters with British bed and breakfasts just wouldn't have been funny if he had been used to them. Part of what delighted a British audience was recognizing the bad food, rude landlords and grim décor – and realizing that somehow we had grown accustomed to and accepted all this shoddiness. There was also an amused recognition that, despite it all, the British would never do anything as American as a making a complaint. Affectionately pointing out a country's foibles and shortcomings is a way in which the travel writer can build an audience within the country they are writing about. People do not like to be criticized, but they do enjoy someone coming in from outside and pointing out what torments they have to put up with – be it bad government or bad vegetable cookery.

Write down all your first impressions as soon as possible. Later, you may find that you have misunderstood something, or find a person's character is more important than their immediately startling face. It can be interesting to go back and use your early notes to build a picture of a person or place as he or it revealed himself or itself to you, going back and admitting that your first impression was deceptive and explaining why.

MAKING NOTES

Making notes may seem a way to ruin a good, spontaneous adventure, but for most people it is hard to write without notebooks to check on. I remember conversations very well and seldom make notes during them, but I do try to make notes as soon as possible afterwards. Something may seem unforgettable, but, when your mind is being flooded with new experiences, memory space seems to fill up and to delete all manner of important things. It can be quite surprising when you look back over your notebooks and discover what you have forgotten. Often there just isn't time to sit down and write up the events of the day. I tend to jot down headings – bitten by giraffe, ate worms, man with strange hat dancing … so that when there is a moment I can go back and fill in the details. I go back as soon as possible, of course, or I shall have forgotten what the headings were about.

Small tape recorders and notebooks inhibit people. Even where I have set up quite a formal interview, I try to just chat, and then write things down the minute I've left the room. Sometimes, where there is clearly an interview situation, I will take notes because otherwise the person may not feel they are being taken seriously. Or the interview may be about something very specific, so I need notes to remember what questions to ask. If there are going to be names, dates and statistics I need to write them down. These are really matters to play by ear, depending on how reticent your subject is and how much you trust your memory. Generally I feel that the notebook is a barrier. In many situations it is better if people don't know you are writing a book because it may make them speak and behave differently, the way many people act up, or clam up, in front of a camera depending on their personality. But at some point, do make notes.

The work to be done in writing all these notes is one reason why most writers prefer to travel alone. If you are in an expedition you will just have to accept that you might be the least sociable member of the team. A formal expedition is a little different from a journey with friends, because other members of the team will have their own work to do, so you won't seem too cranky. Making other members of the expedition part of the story can work very well. Recording how he torments and irritates his fellow travellers, or vice versa, is a central part of Redmond O'Hanlan's work. Some people travel with a partner. This can work if the unravelling or cementing of the relationship is part of what happens on the described journey.

I prefer to travel alone because I will then make a more determined effort to meet and befriend people in the country I'm in. Perhaps they will become travelling companions, or, in one case, partners, but they are part of the place. They have things to tell me and show me that a friend brought along from home would not know. If you are alone, you aren't chatting about life at home. You are observing and listening. You can forget your home life for a while and absorb the new world in front of you. If you are with a friend or a group, you present a sealed unit. You are less approachable. Alone, especially a woman alone, you are more likely to be spoken to by strangers. This can be a nuisance but often the pest at the time makes a great page of comic dialogue in a book. And the strangers may simply be good-hearted and helpful.

I'd overestimated my skills as a map reader and my strength of leg. The walk started well, Belfast looking very Sunday morning, with shop shutters closed and church doors open. I had to go west, then north, and with a bit of effort I'd make it in about half an hour.

An hour later, I was in the Falls Road, passing the murals and too far west, nowhere near north enough. Two old ladies with small Scottie dogs were talking frantically outside a newsagent. A man with a black eye staggered towards me and asked me for some money to get home, I muttered something into my map and kept walking. Another staggering man with a black eye came past me and didn't ask for money. Perhaps they'd been fighting each other and the second one had got away with the first one's wallet ...

A group of teenaged boys headed towards me, exuberant, and one of them shouted a confirmation of what I was thinking;

'Mornin! We're all still drunk from the night before!' Then he held his arms open wide. 'But we're giving out free hugs.'

I said that was very nice but I didn't need a hug.

'You can see she doesn't,' his friend said. 'She needs directions.'

'Here. I know Belfast very well.' The hugging one grabbed my map.

'Where are you going?'

'Thorndale Avenue.'

'Where?'

'It's off the Antrim Road.'

He frowned at me, confused. 'So you're lost then?'

One of his friends grabbed the map. 'Give us that. You can't even read.'

The friend squinted at the map. 'Where off the Antrim road? That's a long road and miles from here.'

'It's miles', the hugging one confirmed. 'You'll need a taxi. We'll find you a taxi.'

Out of nowhere, one of the old women with Scottie dogs pushed her way into the middle of the boys, demanding, 'Is this wee girl lost? Would you not think to help her instead of standing around?'

'We're helping, we've got her map', a boy protested.

'What would you know about maps? Where is it you want, dear?'

'Thorndale Avenue.'

'Oh, I know Thorndale Avenue.'

'My grandmother used to live there', I said. I was suddenly inspired by a wild notion that if the lady was old she might turn out to have known my Grandmother ...

Belfast was small but not that small.

The boys were losing interest now. One of them handed back the map and said, 'She knows everywhere, she used to be a nurse.'

I was sure this had a logic and thanked them as they drifted off, shouting that they were going down to the town to find some girls to hug.

'Wee skitters', the old lady said. 'Now dear, Thorndale Avenue. I know it very well ...'

Annie Caulfield, *Irish Blood, English Heart, Ulster Fry* (Viking Penguin, 2005)

TRAVELLING FROM THE WOMAN'S POINT OF VIEW

In much of the world people are concerned to see a woman travelling alone. They are curious and usually helpful. You tend to be seen as vulnerable. Families are more likely to take you in; hotel staff are more likely to protect you – or old ladies with small dogs take you on as a rescue mission.

I restrict what I do after dark. If I have to go somewhere in a city that can get dangerous, I tell someone in the place I'm staying where I'm off to and when I expect to be back. I try, if it's affordable, to travel with a taxi driver I think seems trustworthy. Instinct is a good friend. Perhaps mine is finely honed after a life in the big city, but nothing really bad has ever happened to me. The minute I don't like the look of a situation or a person, I'm off.

But sometimes running off isn't an option. I have stayed at an out of the way hotel where I distrusted the landlord so much I pushed the dressing table in front of the door at night. The door being unlocked at about two in the morning proved my instincts were right. The door opened and banged against the dressing table a couple of times, I heard an irritated grunt and the prowler abandoned the mission. I was saved from who knows what by a simple, sturdy piece of bedroom furniture.

In Jordan, I once had to travel alone from Amman to Petra and discovered that the tourist buses have journeys to Petra sewn up. Ordinary buses go to a small town on the other side of the mountains. I arrived in the town just after dark. It was starting to snow. The owner of the only taxi company insisted I travel with his burly son and named a price that was far too high. I really didn't like the look of the son, but I was cold, tired and running late. The best I could do was tell them, several times, that I was in a hurry because someone was waiting for me in Petra. On a remote mountain road, with snow blowing round the car in the dark, the driver stopped and climbed into the back seat. I wasn't quite sure what he was saying but I got the idea. He was far too big for me to imagine I could put up any kind of fight. I leapt out into the road and started screaming at him in such a maniacal, curse-filled rage it frightened him. My voice echoed round the mountains. I knew these mountains seemed empty but were likely to have Bedouin living in them. Although I think it was more the surprise of finding me to be psychotic that sent the driver back to his seat. I scrambled back into my seat panicking that he'd go off without me but he didn't. His sulk for the rest of the journey was tangible. He threw my bag into the road and said something nasty when we reached Petra, but I'd survived, so I couldn't care less what he called me. If in doubt, start shouting.

In the Middle East I was careful to dress modestly, so that, if I was hassled, women or more respectful men would rush at my harasser and shame him. In a few places in the world there are people who assume that Western women are sluts, but there will usually be someone standing nearby who doesn't agree with them, so always voice your protests loudly. I've found that instinct, common sense, furniture moving and screaming like a banshee have been enough to keep me safe so far. A friend of mine once found herself in one of those scary barrios of Rio where, if you pat a toddler on the head, he'll stab you in the leg. Everyone looked intimidating and about to pounce. My friend started talking loudly to herself and waving her arms about in an uncoordinated way. She went right through the barrio like this, unscathed, although several children cried. I've never quite had the nerve to try this trick of acting like the roaming, mad lady, but it's something to keep in the store of tricks for an emergency.

On public transport I try to stick with the women and children. Women have scammed money off me far more effectively than men but I don't feel physically threatened. The advantages of being a female traveller, such as the access to women's lives and the kindness of strangers, have always outweighed the inconveniences for me. Male travellers are more likely to get picked on for a fight, make people nervous and not be offered help. And they can still be sexually assaulted, robbed, scammed and stabbed in the leg. The rest of the problems women encounter, they can encounter in their own country. Obscene remarks and not being taken seriously are not annoyances exclusive to a voyage abroad.

I have been asked several times if I'm like the esteemed television presenter and traveller Judith Chalmers and travel without underwear. No. I'm improving, but I do find it hard not to take a lot of luggage. This is a matter of personal style and taste. I don't like to feel scruffy and dirty, or in danger of exposing myself. And I find the hassle of too much luggage less annoying than wasting time doing laundry. I've also found that in countries where I am meeting people who don't have much, I always end up by giving clothes away, so the more I start off with the greater chance I'll end the journey with something left for myself.

I take some very basic medical supplies – plasters, antiseptic cream and diarrhoea tablets. I was given a portable first-aid kit full of bandages and syringes but lost it somewhere. The adventurous travel writer Tim Cahill once told me that there is no point carrying too much of this kind of thing because, if you are going to get that ill, you're better off going home. He suggests that good travel insurance is more practical. Toilet rolls, antiseptic hand wipes and lots of insect repellent about complete the kit. I always take a small but heavy torch that I've never had to use as weapon but feel reassured by the thought that it is under my pillow. If I am nervous, I sleep with my valuables in the bed with me. I don't use a money belt because a thief will know that that is very likely to be where the money is. I have some money in my pocket, some in a day pack and some emergency money in my suitcase or a hotel safe. Depending on how I feel about the hotel.

I write in small exercise books that can be squashed easily into luggage. They make me look as though I'm simply writing a personal diary, not something intimidating or official. I don't take a laptop as I am often in places where electricity surges and cuts out. I hate to have something with me that I shall worry about having stolen, and most of the time I don't like anything that makes me look as though I am up to something of importance. Unless I'm trying to barge in and interview a president, then I might use a proper reporter's notebook.

I tend to bring more money than I think I shall need. Sometimes I'm too broke to do this but it is a nice feeling to know that there's enough spare for an emergency. Although the whole point of travelling is to push yourself out of your usual habits and your comfort zone, I try to do as much as possible to make myself feel comfortable and safe, and to feel as though I am still myself. The unexpected will happen, but there is no point in deliberately inconveniencing yourself – the journey will do that for you. If getting around, getting enough rest and keeping well become too difficult, how are you going to have a moment's peace to meet anyone or to write?

If you can travel with one set of clothes, eating beef jerky and sleeping under trees, then that's who you are. There's no right or wrong about it. The more you travel, the more you'll find what you need to make yourself function well and write well. There are many questions about the ethics of travel. I expect I am responsible for a disgusting amount of carbon emissions, but I try to make up for this by being a fair traveller in other ways. For instance, I think it is unfair to go to a poor country and expect to live too much like the locals. I am Western so I am relatively wealthy, trying to pretend otherwise feels dishonest and exploitive. The day a Nigerian teenager can turn up in Britain, with next to no money, incorrect papers, one change of clothes and tell the official at Heathrow, 'I just thought I'd potter around, live with the locals and write a book about it.' Then that's the day the attitude of a lot of backpackers, budget travellers and travel writers will seem fair to me. Of course, if you always stay at the best hotels, drive hire cars and don't find out where the locals go to eat, then you are not going to find out much. There is a balance to be struck. Remember, no matter how poor and scruffy you look – you look like a tourist in a lot of the world, and that means wealthy. Unless you are looking poor and scruffy in Monaco, where you'll just be ignored by most people except the police.

In *The Road To Oxiana*, written in the 1930s, writer Robert Byron relates how, after an encounter with a persistent guide in Syria, he resigned himself to being labelled a tourist. He accepted that to the Syrians, a man who was travelling on business would be a rich man but a man like Byron, travelling with no apparent purpose, must be incredibly rich. He saw there was no point getting impatient or reasoning with people who were trying to bleed him dry. He was doing his job, being a tourist; they were doing theirs, making money from tourists.

If you are in a place to work, doing something immediately useful for the community, then you will have a much better and more straightforward involvement with a place. Tourism is still, in most of the world, an activity for the privileged. There is nothing wrong with that, as long as you fairly allow people to make a living out of you. This does not mean you have to be a fool and get fleeced, but just remember time is money, for everyone.

Tormenting The Tourists

In other towns in Italy the people lie around quietly and wait for you to ask them a question or do some overt act that can be charged for – but in Annunciation they have lost even that fragment of delicacy; they seize a lady's shawl from a chair and hand it to her and charge a penny; they open a carriage door, and charge for it; they help you to take off a duster – two cents; brush your clothes and make them worse than they were before – two cents; smile upon you – two cents; bow, with a lick-spittle smirk, hat in hand – two cents; they volunteer all information, such as that the mules will arrive presently – two cents – warm day sir – two cents – take you four hours to make the ascent – two cents. And so they go.

Mark Twain, *The Innocents Abroad* (Chatto & Windus, 1869)

PHOTOGRAPHY, MAPS AND DRAWINGS

I am not a good photographer. I seldom use photographs in my work. I find that taking them sets me apart and can cause an awkwardness in what has been an otherwise casual, friendly situation. However, I do, reluctantly, take photographs with a cheap, idiot-proof camera for a number of reasons. They are useful for newspaper and magazine articles. Sometimes publishers ask for them. More importantly, as I have a poor visual memory, I need them for myself. I can look again at a person or place. I can take my time with finding the best description. I always use a print rather than a digital image so I have something to hold in my hand and contemplate.

If you are a good photographer, that may be another string to your bow. I have found that some magazines and newspapers pay more for a photograph than they do for an article. It is usually better to ask before taking someone's photograph. Some cultures have a horror of their image's being in a stranger's hands; most people just prefer to be asked for the sake of good manners. Occasionally, people have asked me whether I have a camera and then ask to have their picture taken. It can be a nice gift to take a photograph of people who have no access to a camera and then send them copies. I find it sad that when I promise people copies of photographs they don't believe me, having been let down before. I have often come across people whose only photographs of themselves or their family were taken by passing tourists.

If you are an experienced photographer, then you will know to check that your camera can survive the temperatures you are going to be travelling in. Also, you'll know to be sure it is well protected from dust, sand, water and the general rough and tumble of travel. It is usually cheaper and easier to buy film, batteries or whatever you need for the camera before you leave. Otherwise it is inevitable that the one type of battery you need won't be available at your destination.

A map at the front of a travel book is always useful. A professional will probably draw the final version used in the book but it is worth making a rough map yourself. Mark towns and sites you visit and, if you made one or two clear journeys, it is a good idea to trace your route. If the country you are travelling to is fairly obscure, a map that shows where the country is in relation to better-known places is useful. It can help give a sense of the size of the country and suggest which neighbouring countries are an influence, or possibly a threat. For *Show Me the Magic* I was lucky enough to have a stylized map and illustrations provided by the artist who did the cover. This was the publisher's idea. The illustrations were at each chapter heading and gave the book a very attractive layout. If you can draw, it is worth putting in a few illustrations of your own. Even at the manuscript stage they can make your work stand out. Drawing while you are on your journey can be an interesting way to attract people to you. Passers by often come up and comment on what you are doing – it can be a way to make friends. Just make sure that you aren't drawing a military installation or a criminal lair.

RESEARCH AND PREPARATION

How much research you need to do really depends on what your project is. But I do think that reading is essential. Anything – journalism, ornithology, anthropology, sociology – you can lay your hands on to broaden your view. Previous travel writers are important for a portrait of the place in the past and to know what has already been said about it. Novels, plays and poetry written by local writers are a vital source of information to me and a surprising number of them can be tracked down in translation. They tell you of problems, preoccupations and people's dreams. They will give depth to what you will write yourself – you will know more than your own point of view.

If you have a facility for languages then do use it. I have often longed to speak to someone and been frustrated by not knowing a word to communicate with. I speak French, some Spanish and a smattering of Arabic. I try to learn the basic greetings wherever I am but wish I could learn more, more quickly. But you can get by without language. Nerve and a lack of embarrassment about using elaborate and energetic signing can carry you some distance. A notebook for drawings of stick men doing the appropriate things can help. Thumbing though a dictionary can involve people in your problem and shows willing. Try to learn what you can but battle to find ways round language problems rather than deciding not to speak to someone. Or worse, not to go on the journey at all.

Try to allow as much time as you possibly can for your journey. If you are on a quest, try not to press on too relentlessly. Find moments to amble around, having chance meetings and watching the unfamiliar world you are in go by. Finally, don't worry if you are not an efficient and laid-back traveller. That can be part of your style. And even the greatest travellers have their shortcomings. On his way to a wild district of northern Kenya with Wilfred Thesiger, writer Gavin Young was amazed to find Thesiger agitating to get to Heathrow airport three hours early. Thesiger, regarded as one of the most fearless of explorers, was close to a nervous breakdown at the thought of missing a flight.

SOME PRACTICALITIES ON THE BOOK

It is a good feeling to set out on a journey with a book contract in your pocket, but it doesn't always happen. If you have a track record as a journalist, novelist or celebrity from another field, it is more likely that a contract will turn up before you have written a word. Even then, some sort of pitch, even if it is just a page or a long conversation would probably be needed. Already well established as a journalist and broadcaster, Mark Lawson received his commission for *The Battle for Room Service* by default. He had always wanted to write a travel book but was held back by what he describes as; 'my wimp illness'. He was courted by commissioning editors, they took him out for meals and suggested trips he might take. All the trips sounded dangerous or at least very uncomfortable. Although a great admirer of intrepid travellers, Lawson knew that just reading their adventures terrified him. Drinking sambuca after one long lunch, Lawson explained his cowardice to an editor and concluded, sadly, that the only journey he could really make was to 'all the safe places'. And so, with another round of sambucas the editor decided to commission Lawson to write *The Battle for Room Service, Journeys to All the Safe Places*.

Not all of us will be taken out for a sambuca and courted to write a book. If a publisher knows, however, that you, a perfectly average person who has never been on television, have had an extraordinary experience and can string a decent sentence together, you could well get a commission without writing the whole book. If you have a very good idea and can write that sentence, a commission based on a pitch only could come your way.

YOUR PRESENTATION

The importance of writing a good opening has already been mentioned. It is also important to write your presentation or pitch for the book in a way that grabs attention, shows that you can write and that there will be enough material to sustain a book. The pitch should begin with a page that summarizes the plan for a book. It should be written in an interesting way, to show your writing voice as well as your selling skills. A sample chapter should follow. This could be the first chapter, or perhaps what you feel will be the most exciting, amusing or moving chapter in the book. Next, there should be a clear outline, several pages long, of what you intend to do for the rest of the book. One way to show you really have a plan for a book rather than a journey is to write a paragraph on what you hope to cover in each chapter. The document should at least show that you have a clear idea of the shape the book will take. Finally, a relevant CV should be attached.

Although I was invited to write my first book, my second one, *The Winners' Enclosure*, was sold on the basis of a pitch. The editor hadn't read my first book. I had never been to Australia. I wrote a comical chapter about the mythology in my family, and many Irish families, concerning lost relatives who had gone to Australia to make good. I did some research about the Irish in Australia and planned a shape for the book, based on tracking significant Irishmen's lives down under. I suggested that there was a good market for the book in Britain, Australia and possibly in Irish America. The publisher of *The Winners' Enclosure* had possible markets in mind, but she told me she bought the book because the first chapter really made her laugh.

Before I was commissioned to write *Show Me the Magic*, I went on a two-week scouting adventure to Benin and found enough to write a sample chapter and a plan for the book. I wrote about my initial encounter with Voudou and, with some research in the library back home, made a plan to investigate Benin and Voudou. This was sold to an editor who hadn't read my previous books and had a limited interest in my previous writing experience. For her, the sale was made on the strength of what she had on the page in front of her. For the next book, about my birthplace Northern Ireland, I knew I had a great deal of material already. Again I wrote a first chapter before making the journey. I wrote it around my sunny childhood memories of Northern Ireland and the contrast with the Northern Ireland on the news. I used as much humour as possible, to show that this would not be the usual, gloom-laden book about the province.

So the rules for the average, non-famous person writing a book pitch are: show that you have a great idea or have had an astounding experience. Show you can write. Show you have everything planned and can sustain a book. Usually a pitch, including a pithy sample chapter, should be about twenty pages long. It should look attractive, with well-spaced type and easy to handle binding. The looks should not matter, but they do. When someone has a lot to read they will pick the manuscript that isn't a challenge to decipher and hold together first out of the pile on their desk, and won't be irritated with you before they have started reading. You could include photographs or drawings if they are going to feature in the book, but otherwise at this stage they are only really useful to catch the eye. Who do you send the pitch to? The first mailing should be to an agent. All but my first book were sold by my agent who knew the specializations, tastes and budgets of various publishers. A known agent's name moves a manuscript up a publisher's reading pile. And many publishers will no longer accept books that are not sent through an agent.

AGENTS AND PUBLISHERS

The bibles for getting started as a writer are *The Writer's Handbook* (Macmillan) or *The Writers' and Artists' Yearbook* (A. &. C. Black). Updated every year, these list agents and their interests. Many agents also list their existing clients, indicating the type of writer they represent. If they represent a well-known travel writer, however, they may not want another. If they do not represent a travel writer they may be interested in taking on a good one, or it could be a form of book they cannot abide. If in doubt, write a short letter or email to the agent to ask.

Agents do tend to specialize because they need to focus their energies on building up contacts and knowledge in particular fields, so looking at their list of interests is more important than their existing client list. J.K. Rowling's agents list themselves as not representing children's books. They do not need another Harry Potter and, having been deluged by pitches for new Harrys, they had to pull up the drawbridge. Publishers know that if an agent has taken on a book then some quality control has already been exercised. There are so many manuscripts and book pitches out there that to try to struggle through without an agent is really difficult. An agent will make sure that you are paid fairly and that your contract doesn't grab all your rights. He or she will nag the publisher to promote your book and throw their own ideas into the marketing effort.

The Writer's Handbook and *The Writers' and Artists' Yearbook* have all kinds of useful information about publishers as well as agents. If you do become impatient with the struggle to find an agent, then looking through the *Handbook* or *Yearbook* for publishers who will take direct submissions from authors is another way forward. Usually these will be small and/or new imprints who may not pay much, but will work hard on the marketing front. Although the way I've described presenting a book proposal is the more usual approach, what publishers require does vary. The publishers' entries in the *Handbook* or *Yearbook* will explain their submission policy. It is also worth checking the publishers' websites where they generally detail their preferred approach. Small publishers, because they are fighting to make money from every book, tend to have far tougher contracts than the large houses. If you cannot get an agent to take you on, it is worth writing to ask one whether they will advise you on a contract, for a five or ten per cent fee.

It may seem odd that an agent would only advise on your contract and not want to represent you. If you have sold a book yourself, an agent may look at you in a different light, but they may still feel reluctant to take on your whole career. They could still feel your writing is not to their taste but, as you're charming, persistent or a friend of a friend, they will help out. If you do not have such useful friends of friends, joining the Society of Authors may be advisable. They produce guidelines and booklets to help with a range of matters concerning authors' rights, so you can get an idea of what not to sign away. For additional information on agents and publishers the internet search engines are very helpful. If you come across a small publisher you have never heard of, the chances are they will not be in any handbooks yet but may have a lively website explaining their policy. Be confident in your covering letter and your pitch, but don't overdo it. No hard sell. Nobody likes a show off.

THE MARKET

The market for travel writing has changing fashions. Ten years ago, largely inspired by the success of Bill Bryson and Pete McCarthy, the trend was for satiric and comical travel writing. Now the fashion is for books about people setting up home and creating alternative lifestyles abroad, following the success of writers such as Carol Drinkwater and Chris Stewart. A regular look through the non-fiction bestseller lists will give you an idea of what is the current craze. Books about setting up alternative lifestyles in southern Europe, particularly around the Mediterranean or anywhere in Spain, have been popular and stuff the shelves. The British desire to follow a dream abroad is still in full flood but shifting to Croatia, Bulgaria, Hungary ... Where else are they going? More importantly, where else are they going that has not been written about yet? A little market research and a few statistics in the back of your proposal won't do your pitch any harm. Similarly if you are a cyclist, caravanner, skier, sailor or skateboarder, adding in figures about how many people share your interest and can't find a thing to read will help your case.

You may wish to shade your pitch to fit in with the current bestselling trends in the genre. Or you may feel that your story can stand alone. Or even create a new trend. What is fashionable when you start writing may have become old hat by the time you publish, so, as always, it is better to be a leader than a follower. There is a steady market for good travel writing that does not reach blockbuster-level sales, just as there is a market for literature that will not be on the supermarket shelves.

It is important to be realistic about how much of publishing is about sales. To consider what will sell does not make you less of a writer. Being sensitive and shrewd are, after all, part of what you need for the writing itself. Use the same skills to develop your idea as you would use in the writing – keep your eyes and ears open. Where are people going all of a sudden? What are large numbers of people doing that they never did before? What would people like to know more about that will involve some interesting travels for you? The more you can back up your fight to get published by being an expert in your chosen field or well known in another, the better, but, it will be the quality and freshness of your book proposal that will attract an agent or publisher. Beyond these is another hurdle – impressing the big booksellers. Agents have to convince editors, who have to convince their sales departments, who have to convince the bookshop chains. This is not just about money. The bookshop chains want to see sales but they also have to hedge their bets – if they exclude someone from their shelves who then goes on to win the Man Booker Prize and the Nobel Prize for literature they could look tawdry and foolish. They could lose out on sulking, big-name authors willing to take part in signings in their store. Although they may have a rush of sales of a novelty book or a reality TV star's memoirs, they have to remember that the steady buyers of books throughout the year are, oddly enough, literate and fairly discerning.

If a book is well reviewed and the word of mouth about it is good, it can become a bestseller without the big stores. The internet is out there now. Bookstores have to watch carefully that they do not make the mistakes of the music industry. While the record stores were nervous of the independent, quirky artists, internet downloads were making stars of mavericks and original voices. At the moment, however, on the traditional route to getting a book on the shelves, publishers have to worry about the bookshops on the high street more than in cyberspace. This may be a situation that changes with the internet refreshing and changing the market. There is commercialization and cynicism in publishing and bookselling, but good books still win through, sometimes. If all the people who work as literary agents, publishers and booksellers were only interested in making money, most of them would be working elsewhere.

For agents and publishers there is a balance to maintain between working enthusiastically for love and being realistic. The same applies to writers.

Booksellers and publishers should be given credit for having a fair idea of customer demand. It is up to the writer to study the market. The authors who complain most are in two categories: those who cannot bring themselves to believe that what sold ten years ago does not necessarily sell now and those who slavishly follow a current fashion only to find that by the time they get in on the act, the market has moved on.

The secret is to find an original idea which fits into one of the identifiable market sectors. As a formula for literary success this may be irritatingly vague but no one ever said it was easy and if it was, the market would be swamped and we would be back at square one trying to find an identifiable voice that somehow could be heard above all others.

Barry Turner, *The Writer's Handbook* (Macmillan, 2007)

OTHER MARKETS

NEWSPAPERS AND MAGAZINES

The internet is bringing great changes, but there are already other places for travel writers to sell their work, such as newspapers, magazines, radio and television. The travel supplements of most newspapers depend on freelancers to help to fill their pages. They don't have enough money to send teams of staff around the world to write all the articles and take all the pictures they need. All newspapers have different tones of voice and target markets. Study their travel supplements to see whether your style and your piece fit in.

The first thing to notice is that the style of writing in most newspapers and magazines is not the same as that used in writing a travel book. Travel books are anecdotal, personal – they tell a story. Articles are largely descriptive. What is a place like? Who goes there? How do I get there? What is there to do when I'm there? Travel pages and supplements are read by people thinking of taking a holiday. For this reason the supplements print only occasional features on strange and far-flung places. These articles on unusual destinations are very often by well-known authors who lend kudos to the paper, or will be read for their own sake. This leaves a wealth of destinations that need to be written about for the summer holiday market, weekend break market and the winter sun or skiing holiday enthusiast. The familiar destinations can always be looked at with fresh eyes. Where is there a good beach in Spain that has been forgotten about? What is an interesting new route to drive around the Italian lakes? What peculiar new theme park have you discovered in Florida? Is there a new diving centre in Malta? As a travel writer you may feel your trip has been rather touristy, but that does not mean you won't sell a piece on it. Travel editors are desperate for a new angle on the Costa Blanca, Italy, Cyprus, Malta, Florida ... If a new resort is opening up, or an old resort has been neglected, that is the stuff of travel pages.

Have you travelled with teenagers, small children, elderly relatives, pets or a caravan? All these are the accompaniments to many people's travels. There is always a need for suggestions, advice and practical insider tips. Wherever tourists go, travel editors will need regular new articles on those destinations. It is quite possible to start your travel writing career with a piece on

Torremolinos. Travel supplements have existing columns that you could write a piece for. Do they need city break pieces? Travel with children pieces? Cheap travel pieces? Package holiday reports? If you are not sure whether the paper or magazine takes freelance contributions for their regular columns, ring the travel editor and ask. They may be irritable, I know several who are, but they can't bite you. And mostly they welcome a freelancer who tries to fit in with what the paper needs rather than sending them 2,000 words on backpacking in Burkina Faso. Make notes on prices, airlines, hotels and vaccination and visa requirements. Some papers do their own fact checking but you may be asked to do it.

Papers may use stock photographs from picture libraries, but, if you can provide your own, that is an extra credit and payment for you. High quality, glossy magazines, whose photographic content is part of why they are purchased, still ask for transparencies. But for newspapers a well-lit, clearly defined print or emailed digital image will work as well in these days of scanners and downloads. Most now prefer colour to black and white. Again, your *Writer's Handbook* is useful to tell you whether a paper or magazine takes freelance copy and how it would like it to be submitted. Email is taking over from hard copy, but do ensure that you submit it in an attachment that can be opened by most PCs. Write a short covering letter, summarizing your piece in one concise sentence – a child-friendly cruise in the Mediterranean; canoeing holidays in Germany; diving in South Africa.

The next thing is then to leave well alone for a couple of weeks. Editors are busy and need some time to get to the contributions of freelancers. On the other hand, a telephone call after a couple of weeks may move you towards the top of the pile. A little skill is needed in the call; life at a newspaper is all hassle and so if you sound like a hassler, an editor will rapidly go off you. Ask very, very pleasantly, whether the idea of the piece would be interesting to them, should you wait until they have had a chance to read it or would they advise you to try elsewhere? Never threaten to go elsewhere because, frankly, who cares if you do when there are hundreds of unsolicited pieces in the inbox? Sound eager to please but not pushy; affable, but businesslike. It is best not to leave a message for someone to call you back, the chances that they will are very remote. You could be hassle. I am sure that you are perfectly capable of telephoning an editor and sounding pleasant without my pointing out that this is the best way to proceed – but I have been asked a number of times whether editors should be approached with a 'hard sell'. You do need to be bold, but there is no need to turn into an aggressive maniac to sell your article. The longest articles in newspapers or magazines are usually no more than 2,500 words, and these longer pieces are generally done in-house or by recognized authors. What editors love is short, pithy pieces to fill the awkward spaces on their pages – a thousand words, 800 or 500 will sell far more easily than long pieces.

What should the article be like? Pack in practical information suitable for the target audience but don't be dull; if you can include some humour, a relevant quotation or a small personal introduction it will bring an informative piece to life; for instance: 'I'd always thought Ibiza was for teenage ravers; I'm definitely not one of those but had an interesting weekend that involved no dancing, ecstasy nor group sex.' Whether or not you mention group sex does depend on the publication you are aiming at. You don't have to find an unusual destination, just an unusual take on it. What are summer resorts like off-season? Have you found something for the under twenty-fives in a destination usually associated with pensioners? Keep thinking and keep it brief.

A much overlooked section in many newspaper supplements are the pages devoted to holidays in the British Isles. Writing for these sections may not involve the exotic travel you hoped for, but it may be a way to pay a few bills and start building your writing contacts and CV. There are seaside resorts, country houses, industrial museums, cathedrals, city farms, canal trips ... Global warming, screaming children, shortage of time and money mean that there are crowds of people looking for a holiday that does not involve flying far away. You may just need to walk to the end of your road – is there a sight in your own town that tourists from abroad flock to see? Is there some bizarre cheese-rolling festival that could make an interesting day out? Start with that.

Glossy magazines tend to commission their pieces from in-house or well-known writers. If you feel your piece suits a magazine it is still worth ringing to ask whether they would be interested. You may have gained access to a Libyan archaeological site that few have visited, have wonderful photographs and political insight that will get you through the eye of the glossy magazine needle. Don't forget to be sure that you have read the magazine and know that it is the sort of article they print. Specialist magazines for particular age and interest groups are often easier to sell to than the mainstream glossies. People forget to submit their work outside the main papers and magazines on the newsagents' stands but *The Writer's Handbook* lists dozens of publications that you may never have thought of. These may have a decent circulation and probably pay only a little less than some of the broadsheets.

THE INTERNET AND RESEARCH

It is always worth trawling the internet for new magazine titles or internet travel sites. Some of the sites pay and have a wide audience. Writing for the internet requires a very concise style. People tend to let their eyes drift across internet articles, so short paragraphs, very much to the point and moving swiftly on, are the way to construct your article. Pithy anecdotes, facts and figures leap off the screen more readily than descriptive passages or meditative writing. Many web articles are broken up with subheadings and have lists of bullet points. Research shows that these suit the glancing way people read on-screen. There is an impatience in the way people do this, so anything to pull them up short is useful, a startling fact or sharp change of direction will refocus the reader's concentration, but using complicated sentences with several clauses will lose the reader's attention. Writing on the web is to write for people in a hurry who are looking to find something out or be quickly entertained. Some useful travel writing sites, although typing in 'travel writing' will add to this list and make sure you are up to date, are listed at the back of this book. Also, look for individual writers' websites, Peter Moore has a very good one, full of advice and encouraging interaction.

To research a print magazine a survey of its website can give a thorough background to what its aims and requirements are. Although most magazines prefer a descriptive piece – 'what to do when you get to Bali' type of article – there are exceptions. The travel magazine *Wanderlust* takes the sort of writing more usually found in travel books; they want anecdotal, high quality personal accounts of unusual journeys, but magazines such as *National Geographic* require a very specialized knowledge of your destination; their brief is still to show the reader places, people and animals that not easily accessible or are part of a disappearing world and they also publish pieces on matters of technological interest, such as the engineering involved in the rebuilding of the Panama Canal. They have limited openings for freelancers but a specialist piece stands more chance; fossils, restoration and conservation are strong themes to approach them with. Submit something you feel is suitable and let them know where you plan to go or what project you will be working on next. It may be that your writing and photography are impressive enough and your piece is unusual enough to have them take an interest.

To recap, research the style of the paper or magazine, preferably reading several issues so that you have a clear idea of their style and typical content. Be persistent but not too pushy. Some editors will sound vague in their refusal because they don't like to be rude. To clarify this you could ask what kind of thing they are looking for, thus forcing them to admit that they don't like your writing or don't feel that it suits the publication. For the most part, be brief. There are more slots for 500 words than for pieces over a thousand. It is better to have an editor ask you to extend a piece than to have it get into print but slashed to half the size in a way that makes you weep. All these print and internet outlets are ways to earn a little money and build up a readership. This shows a professionalism to agents and book editors and keeps your name in the public eye if you haven't yet had a book published or if you haven't published a book for several years. Short trips to scout ideas for a book may tell you that there is not enough material to make a book from after all, but there will certainly be an article to be written.

RADIO

The first articles I sold were to radio. There was a BBC programme, now defunct, with a producer very interested in getting travellers who were not journalists to contribute to it. That programme has gone, but similar ones have replaced it. The main outlets are the BBC World Service and BBC Radio 4. Listen for the name of the producer at the end of the programme, or look in *Radio Times* where producers' names are usually listed. A short piece on one programme could lead to something longer, until finally you will have built up enough of a reputation to get them to trust you with a whole programme. Anecdote and reported dialogue work better on radio than description or statistics. Use simpler sentences than you would in print. 'However' and 'nevertheless' are the kinds of word to avoid, not only do listeners lose the sense of a long sentence but the person reading will lose energy too. Most importantly, always read the work aloud to yourself several times, checking that you haven't produced some tongue twisters or words that may not look ambivalent but do sound it. A short, clear piece of no more than 800 words submitted to a programme that has writers read their own work could be the start of a radio career.

'From Our Own Correspondent' uses freelance pieces that are particularly suited to travel writers because they take the form of a short story rather than a report. 'From Our Own Correspondent' pieces are always exactly 800 words long. One of these takes nearly two minutes to read, a very long time in radio. For most other programmes, 200 or 300 words will be enough. If the producer likes your piece, he may ring you to hear your voice as much as to find out who you are. You do not need to have a mellifluous actor's voice, just speak clearly and slowly; if your voice is reasonable and you don't freeze with fright in front of a microphone most producers are used to giving a little vocal coaching. Again, research is the key. Listen to the programmes, find the names of the producers and, if in doubt, ring up and ask whether they take freelance pieces and how they would like them to be submitted. After some programmes you will hear the name of an independent production company. These are often small and approachable, but they have to sell their material to the broadcaster, usually the BBC. It is unlikely that they will risk trying to sell a programme from an unknown writer and presenter, but, if they like your writing, like you and think you have enough talent to carry a programme, they may take a risk.

If you are an expert on, for instance, an ecological project in the Orkneys, where you have been working and getting to know people for months, then you stand a reasonable chance of offering your programme as the writer and presenter. If you have only heard about this project and done some cursory research on the internet, then you are not locking yourself into the project enough. Try to make sure that you not only present a great idea but make yourself clearly indispensable to the programme. The more focused your idea is, the more likely it is to get used. If you have found an extraordinary person or organization, try to write a tight piece on him or it, using quotations wherever possible. It may be that you will be sent out to conduct an interview, but for the purposes of writing the piece for radio, quotations liven up the prose; for instance, '"I've been keeping bats in Margate for twenty-five years", George tells me.' This is a more lively start to a piece than, 'I met a man called George who had been keeping bats in Margate for twenty-five years.' For radio, write in the present tense. Make the listener feel that they are standing with you while you talk to George. Asides about the history of bat keeping in Margate can go into the past tense, of course, but as much as possible, keep a sense of immediacy. If you are sent out to interview George, radio equipment is small and simple to use. No one will send you out without giving you some technical tips. If George waffles or you fluff a question, editing back at the studio will save you. If you are asked to report live on George and you make a mistake, keep going. If George gets boring, interject a firm and definite question.

You may feel that you want to concentrate on travel writing and that radio is not relevant to you. It's just worth bearing in mind that many of the people you will meet in radio also have contacts in the print media or in countries you might want to visit with a plan to write something. Anything you learn about how to interview people and make a piece for radio come alive is very useful when you get back to researching and writing for books and articles.

PRESENTING

Presenting is a skill in itself but it is a useful way for a writer to get known and to sell books. If you feel that you could manage it, it is well worth a try. I haven't learnt much yet, but what I do know is to keep your energy levels up and keep talking. Be relaxed and imagine that you are talking to a friend rather than addressing the nation. Even if you have no interest in becoming a presenter, it is likely that when you are promoting a book you will be interviewed. If you are lively and full of ready anecdotes, it will attract people to your book. If you give gruff, 'yes' and 'no' answers, the interviewer will spend the shortest time possible with you and people will barely have a chance to hear about your book. If you get a reputation as a monosyllabic interview subject the chances are that, no matter how fascinating it is, you won't be asked back to talk about your next book. If you are pleasant company for the interviewer and make their lives easy by having plenty to say in a relaxed manner, then they will give you a good amount of time on their programme, and they will remember you as a good bet for next time.

Broadcasting and presenting skills are something you learn as you go along. It is difficult when you are nervous and everything is new to remember that relaxation is the key. If you are relaxed, you will sound more engaging and speak slowly enough. Nerves tend to make people gabble and, on radio, you do need to speak at a slightly slower than natural pace. Not too slowly, of course, or listeners will become impatient and you will sound as though you are bored. Speaking slowly while remaining focused and being energetic is natural to some, but most of us have to learn. To a certain extent it is simply a microphone technique, talking into it as though to a person of whom you are fond, even though they aren't the brightest person you know and need things to be explained very clearly. A studio engineer told me to try this slow-witted, good friend technique and I found that it really helped me to be focused and calm down on the microphone. If you are lucky you will come across people willing to help you in these small, invaluable ways and who are willing to take a chance on you while you are still learning.

Producers willing to take chances are more common in radio than in television. As a speech medium, radio is more suited to writers, but there is less money involved so producers have a lot less fear of wasting tape on you if it turns out that you aren't that all they hoped you would be.

As with newspaper supplements, travel around Britain is worth considering for radio and television. It would be easier to sell a programme on Margate than on the Maldives. Cost is a factor, but also there will be more people competing to get a job in the Maldives than in Margate. So perhaps, if you know Margate, all its quirks and secrets, start there. It will be a stepping stone to the Maldives.

TELEVISION

Television is much harder to break into than radio. The personality of the presenter can make or break a programme. You really need to feel confident that you can pull off an energetic chat to camera before you should even think about trying. It is more likely you will be picked up to present short travel segments on television if you have already been working in radio or print. If you feel that you are bursting with charisma, are articulate and amusing, it may be worth submitting a programme idea based around yourself. Your case for yourself will be enhanced if, not only are you charismatic and articulate, but you are an expert in a particular field. Do you travel the world to track down dangerous snakes? Do you climb impossible mountains or make hazardous dives? Are you one of the few Westerners to speak an obscure Mongolian dialect, or to have studied the temples on a remote island? If you are a specialist, your chances are better. The pitch for your television programme needs to have the kind of hook we were talking about for a book pitch – only more so. The novelty of the idea needs to leap out of the first sentence and the visual possibility of the idea needs to be clear by the second. *The Writer's Handbook* lists the heads of departments of the several television channels. It also lists independent production companies. If a company seem to specialize in travel or factual documentaries it is worth submitting through them. If you have seen their name at the end of a programme you enjoyed then that is a good sign they can get programmes made and could sell your idea to a broadcaster for you. Television is hard to break into but it is always worth being bold. The independent company you befriend may not sell your programme but they may see your worth and take you on as a researcher on another programme. Maybe next time you will be an assistant producer, and then the time after that get one of your own ideas through. Even if you never get in front of a camera, working as a researcher or assistant on travel programmes is a way to see the world at someone else's expense, while doing interesting work and possibly thinking about your next book.

FINDING THE MONEY

The writer Ian Marchant maintains that, 'Mostly, writers are paid in time and freedom.' This particularly applies to travel writers who have to spend a portion of their advances on their fares and accommodation.

Ways to save your advance to feed the children back home are tricky to find. If you are already published or broadcasting, it gets easier. Organizations such the Travel Writers' Guild have discount arrangements and special offers for members, but they let you join only if you are already published. Some travel writers take on an academic mission or scientific research as part of their project and build up some sponsorship that way. There are grants available, particularly for younger writers and *The Writer's Handbook* suggests ways to investigate these. The Society of Authors produces a small guide annually, listing grants and awards. Call them or go to their website to order the latest edition. It is not expensive and is very useful as new grants come up all the time.

If you are going somewhere particularly remote, it may be worth thinking about universities with meteorological, anthropological, medical, geological, zoological or some such department that might give you a little money to do some research for them. Usually you would need some qualification in the field to make the department interested, but it is always worth a few letters and telephone calls presenting yourself as a sensible, responsible person who could collect information for them. If you cycle, dive, skateboard, hike or travel in some way that needs special equipment, it is likely you could convince a company to provide you with free equipment in return for promoting them or testing a product. It is possible to avoid paying your way but often it takes up so much time to save a little money it is barely worth it. I have found that it requires much letter writing and unctuous calls to tourist boards, hotels, airlines, ferry companies and the like to get something for nothing. If a hotel or air route is new or undersubscribed you may get a discount at least. You could simply find the service you get is very eager.

It is never a good idea to promise publicity if you are not certain that you can deliver. I know a number of travel editors who have a blacklist of people who have tried to get free holidays by claiming to be writing an article for their publications. Even where an article has been commissioned, some editors will ask you not to approach people for free accommodation, travel or some other benefit by using the paper's name. Sometimes this is to protect the paper from angry hoteliers blaming the paper for your scathing remarks. Sometimes it is because large organizations should be spending money advertising in the paper rather than taking the cheaper route of a mention in an article.

I tend to prefer getting a publisher, literary festival or broadcaster to pay my way than by my pleading with the hotels or transport organizations myself. For one thing, if I want to write bad things about them it seems like bad manners if I have been given a free ride. I particularly avoid trying to get discounts or free rides in poor countries; I have seen people wave their press badges and intimidate people who can ill afford to give cut-price accommodation, transport or even free entry into a ramshackle museum. To me, this goes beyond bad manners; I suppose that I have a puritanical streak that maintains that, if you cannot afford to pay for something, you cannot have it.

GUIDE BOOKS AND OTHER OPTIONS

Getting the publishers, festivals or broadcasters to pay your way is easier because they usually need you to be somewhere to do your job. Airlines and hotels need cash; they don't need you to do your job, unless you are specifically reviewing them for a paper or guide. If you are working for a well-known guidebook getting things free becomes easier and often more necessary. Most guidebooks will give you a set budget to write the book and usually a limited amount of time to complete it. I know of one budget guide company that pays so little that its writers tend to hang around the lobbies of expensive hotels asking the guests' opinions rather than stay there themselves. Similarly, they will haunt the doorsteps of the more expensive restaurants in a country; they have to report on the fancy places but they aren't given a fancy budget. There are travel writers who make a living by guidebook writing. It is exhausting work and usually done for little profit. Guidebook companies with a strict house style give their writers such a narrow template to work to that it can be frustrating for the imaginative. The work becomes very much writing to order, joining dots and ticking boxes. Nevertheless, if you have the energy and ingenuity, guidebook writing is a way to get to know a country well and have a lot of fun. Perhaps your real writing can come later. You may have the energy to gather information and record anecdotes for yourself as you go along and you may come across a story to return to when you have more time. Travel guides have different styles depending on their target markets. If you know a country well and notice that a particular company does not cover it, it could be worth offering your services. It is more likely that you will find your way in by submitting contributions and updates to existing guidebooks. If these are taken, usually for little or no money, it is worth writing to the company and asking whether they have any vacancies. Many guidebook writers started out by working in the home office of the company, building contacts and listening out for where there might be a guide update needed.

If you have worked as a tour guide, journalist or charity volunteer in a country, guidebooks may take more interest in you than if you are simply an enthusiastic traveller. You need to be able to write quickly and clearly. You will need some investigative skills, and, as you have to move fast, an ability to travel happily alone. If you think a guidebook to a country you know well is woefully out of date, a tactful letter outlining your expertise and asking whether the company is updating the guide could open the door for you. If, of course, you don't use phrases such as 'woefully out of date'.

Giving talks at universities, festivals or to writers' groups is a useful way to promote your book. You are usually paid for the talk and literary festivals, in particular, are often held in attractive surroundings, so the job feels like a holiday in itself. If the thought of public speaking, such as radio or television presenting, fills you with horror, then remember that there are plenty of writers who survive without these platforms. If you are interested, it may be that your publisher's press office will arrange some appearances, but they will work for you only around publication time. In between the rushes of attention when a book is published, public speaking is a way to get out and about and to create some employment that relates to your writing. Send out your CV and a brief outline of a talk or workshop idea to universities with creative writing courses, to writers' groups and to literary festivals. The British Council website has a long list of festivals and such groups. A web search for creative writing courses will suggest places you can offer your services to outside universities, such as arts or adult education centres. Some writers find this kind of self-promotion embarrassing; I find it a way to earn a little extra money, sell books, meet people and see new places, even if it is only a college campus in the West Midlands.

All these asides to literary travel writing are worth considering until you have a bestseller. Or even then, they are a way to keep moving and to keep yourself in the public eye. You might find yourself visiting and writing about somewhere you would never have considered if you hadn't been asked. An entire book can take a long time to research, but writing short pieces in the meantime keeps you in touch with the writer while the traveller is working.

A Typical Travel Writer

No landlord is my friend and brother, no chambermaid loves me, no waiter worships me, no boots admires and envies me. No round of beef or tongue or ham is expressly cooked for me, no pigeon pie is especially made for me, no hotel advertisement is personally addressed to me, no hotel room tapestried with great coats and railway wrappers is set apart for me, no house of public entertainment in the United Kingdom greatly cares for my opinion of its brandy or sherry. When I go upon my journeys, I am not usually rated at a low figure in the bill; when I come home from my journeys, I never get any commission. I know nothing about prices and should have no idea, if I were put to it, how to wheedle a man into ordering something he doesn't want. As a town traveller, I am never to be seen driving a vehicle externally like a young and volatile pianoforte van, and internally like an oven in which a number of flat boxes are baking in layers. As a country traveller, I am rarely to be found in a gig, and am never to be encountered by a pleasure train, waiting on the platform of a branch station, quite a Druid in the midst of a light Stonehenge of samples. And yet – I am both a town traveller and a country traveller, and am always on the road. Figuratively speaking I travel for the great house of Human Interest Brothers, and have rather a large connection in the fancy goods way. Literally speaking, I am always wandering here and there from my rooms in Covent Garden, London – now about the city streets: now about the country bye-roads – seeing many little things, and some great things, which, because they interest me, I think may interest others.

Charles Dickens, *The Uncommercial Traveller* (Chapman and Hall, 1861)

How to Continue

You love to travel, your head is full of stories but you still find it impossible to get writing. The first thing is to make time. Decide that next Sunday morning you will sit down for two hours and write. Just begin. Think about the last trip you made and write down everything you can remember about the first day. Don't apply any quality control to this. Just keep writing, rambling on, until you reach the end of the day. There will be long passages you cannot decipher, lots of repetition, paragraphs where every second phrase seems to be 'and then' but you will have filled some pages. Then go back over it, beginning to trim it, crossing out repetition and moments that are not really very interesting. Write it all out again in this honed-down version. Read through, looking for places to improve descriptions, add dialogue or lose the more flagging paragraphs. You may need to write it all out yet again before getting to your goal, a finely-honed 500 words. Then, within a morning or a couple of mornings, you will have an article.

Writing classes and courses can be another way to force yourself to start. I do recommend finding a tutored class or course rather than a group where everyone is a beginner reading their work to each other. I think these groups can be too competitive and unstructured. A tutor may not be very good, but there is more chance of their advice and opinion being valuable than that of a fellow beginner. You may disagree with the tutor and find them too judgmental, but don't let that put you off. It is only their opinion. Perhaps try another course or carry on regardless once you have used the course to get you putting words on paper.

The internet is a good place to find local travel-writing classes or courses. The Arvon Foundation sometimes runs travel or non-fiction writing courses. Find out who the tutor is and what they have done. This way you can feel a little confident in their opinions or suggestions. The main thing is not to look for praise or criticism but to use the class or course to start getting words on to paper and being bold enough to make them public. The nerve-racking experience of reading aloud in front of a small group will be good practice for all those difficult calls to agents and editors ahead of you.

Once you have started, keep going. Make more and more time for yourself to write every day. Even if you cannot give up the day job yet and cannot bring yourself to sell the children on E-bay, there will be 15 minutes you can find in which to write a diary or add a few sentences to a story. Think of writing as exercise. A short stint in the gym every day is better than 2 hours once a month.

If you have finished a manuscript or an article and sent it out, don't sit back. It could be the second, third … or tenth thing you write that sells. Once you start selling, it would be good to have a store of material built up to draw on. And to have got into the discipline of writing every day as your efforts turn into a career. It is as difficult to sustain a career in writing as it is to get started. Even if you have a bestseller you may feel you want to write a book every few years. The subsequent books may not sell as well. There are few writers who have everything they write turn into gold. This is why some of the asides such as article writing and public speaking are valuable for those who want to keep working, regardless of how much money they have made.

TOMORROW

Keeping your ears and eyes open for forgotten places and overlooked routes will always be important. Keeping up with new magazines, websites and radio programmes is just as important as researching new journeys. The world changes all the time and so does the market for travel writing. When you begin to be established it is worth joining professional organizations. These can be a source of work to back up the efforts of your agent. They can also be a way to find out what is happening in publishing or broadcasting. They can simply be a way to meet other writers. Try not to get too bogged down in worrying about selling your work and making a career before you have even started. In the beginning, it is important to develop your story-telling voice. If you have a friend just back from holiday, you don't really want to hear about exactly how high the Taj Mahal is or exactly how much water flows over the Niagara falls – what you want them to give you is a sense of how those places made them feel; you want to hear flavoursome anecdotes about their travels and their entertaining or moving personal encounters. You want them to fill you with wonder, laughter and sadness about the big world out there and how many different ways people find to live in it. This is good storytelling.

Travel writing does need new kinds of voice. There is still a need for non-European takes on the world, women writers and writers who have new or expert thoughts on countries that have been closed off by politics or have suddenly been changed. The change could be a political revolution or an ecological disaster. Change does not have to mean big, sudden news, thus there has been a gradual surge in expatriate living in Europe and the revitalizing of the ocean cruise holiday to inspire recent travel writers. What's the next big change?

People are busy, they cannot go everywhere themselves but would be sorry if travel writers weren't continually heading off and coming back with stories. The snapshots of the past contained in the work of long-dead travel writers do need to be added to by today's stories of a changing world. The big stuff, the news, will go into the history books. The travel writers will preserve details of the ordinary people living in the spaces between the headlines – the little secrets of the world.

The world is not so small ... one of many unusal sights seen by the author on her travels in Benin. (Photo: Annie Caulfield)

BIBLIOGRAPHY

FURTHER READING

Bell, Gertrude, *The Desert and the Sown* (Heinemann, 1907)
de Botton, Alain, *The Art of Travel* (Hamish Hamilton, 2002)
Bryson, Bill, *Neither Here Nor There* (Minerva, 1991)
Byron, Robert *The Road to Oxiana* (1937, new ed. Pimlico, 2004)
Cahill, Tim, *Pecked to Death by Ducks* (Fourth Estate, 1993)
Cahill, Tim, *Road Fever* (Fourth Estate, 1992)
Chatwin, Bruce, *What Am I Doing Here?* (Jonathan Cape, 1989)
Caulfield, Annie, *Irish Blood, English Heart, Ulster Fry* (Viking Penguin, 2005)
Caulfield, Annie, *Kingdom Of The Film Stars* (Lonely Planet, 1997)
Caulfield, Annie, *Show Me the Magic* (Viking Penguin, 2002)
Caulfield, Annie, *The Winners' Enclosure* (Simon and Schuster, 1999)
Davidson, Basil, *Africa in History* (Wiedenfeld & Nicholson, 2001)
Dew, Josie, *The Sun in My Eyes* (Time Warner, 2001)
Drysdale, Helena, *Dancing with the Dead* (Hamish Hamilton, 1991)
Drysdale, Helena, *Looking for George* (Picador, 1996)
Equiano, Olaudah, *The Interesting Narrative* (Modern Library Classics, 2004)
Eshun, Echow, *Black Gold of the Sun* (Hamish Hamilton, 2005)
Fryer, Peter, *Staying Power: The History of Black People in Britain* (Pluto Press, 1984)
Gellhorn, Martha, *The View from the Ground* (Granta Books, 1989)
Hawks, Tony, *Playing the Moldovans at Tennis* (Ebury Press, 2001)
Hawks, Tony, *Round Ireland with a Fridge* (Ebury Press, 1999)
Joris, Lieve, *Gates of Damascus* (Lonely Planet, 1996)
Joris, Lieve, *Mali Blues* (Lonely Planet, 1997)
Kennedy, A.L., *On Bullfighting* (Yellow Jersey Press, 1999)
Lawson, Mark, *The Battle for Room Service: Journeys to All the Safe Places* (Picador, 1993)
Linqvist, Sven, *Desert Divers* (Granta Books, 2000)
Linqvist, Sven, *Exterminate all the Brutes* (Granta Books, 1997)
Mercer, Jeremy, *Books, Baguettes and Bedbugs* (Orion, 2005)
Moore, Peter, *Same Same but Different* (Amazon Shorts, 2006)
Morris, Jan, *A Sultan in Oman* (Faber & Faber, 1957)
O'Hanlan, Redmond, *Trawler* (Hamish Hamilton, 2003)
Phillips, Caryl, *The European Tribe* (Faber & Faber, 1987)
Pritchett, V.S., *The Spanish Temper* (Chatto & Windus, 1954)
Raban, Jonathan, *Sea Room* (Granta Books, 1984)
Raban, Jonathan, *The Journey and the Book* (The New York Times, 1981)
el Saadawi, Nawal, *My Travels around the World* (Methuen, 1991)
Seal, Jeremy, *Santa – A Life* (Picador, 2005)
Sackville-West, Vita, *Passenger to Tehran* (Penguin Books, 1943)

Said, Edward, *Culture and Imperialism* (Vintage, 1994)

Sillitoe, Alan, *The Blind Leading the Blind: A Century of Guidebook Travel (1815–1911)* (Macmillan, 1996)

Soutter, Andy, *Australiaville* (Abacus, 1996)

Stewart, Chris, *Driving Over Lemons* (Sort Of Books, 1999)

Tacitus [AD55–c.118], *Agricola and Germania* (trans. H. Mattingly and S.A. Handford, Penguin Classics, 1973)

Theroux, Paul, *Sunrise with Seamonsters* (Penguin Books, 1985)

Turner, Barry, *The Writer's Handbook* (Macmillan, 2007)

Twain, Mark, *The Innocents Abroad* (Chatto & Windus, 1869)

Young, Gavin, *Return To The Marshes* (Hutchinson, 1981)

Young, Gavin, *Worlds Apart* (Penguin Books, 1987)

Writers' and Artists' Yearbook (A & C Black, 2007)

TRAVELLING IN CYBERSPACE

Some of these websites may prove useful. Writers' own websites as well as the sites for publishers and agents can also provide insights or quick answers to your questions.

Organizations

bgtw.org (British Guild Of Travel Writers)
rgs.org (Royal Geographical Society)
societyofauthors.net

Courses

arvonfoundation.org
author-network.com
writers-circles.com/travel

Magazines and Online Writing Advice/Opportunities

adventuretravelwriter.com
bootsnall.com
geographical.co.uk
transitionsabroad.com
travelinsights.com
travelintelligence.com
travel-quest.co.uk
travellerstales.org
travelwriters.com
wanderlust.co.uk
worldrover.net
writing.org

Travel Advice and Working Abroad

gapyear.com
travellers.com
travellersworldwide.com
vso.org.uk
workingabroad.com

INDICES

INDEX OF PEOPLE